New advanced vocabulary
Palabra por Palabra
Spanish

Phil Turk

Introduction

This 3rd Edition of *Palabra por Palabra* contains yet more words and phrases arranged by topic, with the *Ciencia y tecnología* and *Trabajo* chapters being much extended to provide a wide range of IT vocabulary and useful phrases for the workplace. Some chapters have been arranged into a more logical order, phrases which have become current since the last edition have been added and areas of vocabulary which seemed no longer relevant have been discarded.

Some of the vocabulary is contextualised in short 'off-the-shelf' phrases, and can be used as such. You can also adapt them as necessary to fit other contexts. Many of the words and phrases have been taken from magazines or newspapers and are therefore totally authentic. Others are the result of consultations with native Spanish speakers to find the equivalents of common phrases that occur in the English-speaking media.

The topics covered will be very useful for students tackling the revised AS and A2 specifications from 2000, as well as other students at a similar level of Spanish. At the end of most chapters you will find website addresses (both Spanish and Spanish American) which are a useful source for obtaining more information – and therefore more vocabulary – about aspects of the topic in question.

Learning vocabulary

As an advanced language student, you will by now be aware that words are the tools of the trade. However sound your knowledge of grammar and facts, and however brilliant your ideas, you cannot express them without the necessary words! And unlike when you learnt your mother tongue, unless you are very lucky, you won't be surrounded by people around you speaking Spanish all hours of your waking day. More likely your contact will be limited to a few hours of Spanish classes a week. Try, however, to increase your contact through websites, any newspapers, magazines or other materials in Spanish you can get hold of, your dictionary, and TV satellite programmes if you can receive them. We have provided you with a good selection of words and phrases on most of the topics you are likely to encounter, but you should also keep your own vocabulary notebook and jot down, as far as possible under topic headings, any further ones you come across.

Vocabulary learning is a very personal process and each of us will discover the method that suits us best. However, you must accept that it won't 'stick' without some effort on your part. The important thing is to experiment and find the method that works best for *you*! And, by the way, 'method' is the key word: you must be *methodical*! Try this...

● Find somewhere quiet: turn off that CD player!

- Decide which area of vocabulary you wish to concentrate on. (It should preferably be one you have been studying in class, so at least some of the words should be familiar, if not fully fixed in your mind!)
- Don't try to learn too much at once.
- By now you will probably have some idea how much you can absorb in one go: it's unlikely to be more than 30 words or phrases, maybe only 20.
- Take the first 10 words/phrases, read them through 3 times with the English.
- Cover the Spanish with a piece of paper and try the first one.
- Reveal the Spanish: did you get it right? If so, put a tick against it.
- Repeat for all 10 words.
- Now take a further 10 and repeat the process (and a further 10 if your target is 30).
- TAKE A BREAK.
- After that, come back to your vocabulary and repeat the process for each of the groups of 10 words: put a second tick against each word you get right.
- Keep on repeating this process at intervals until you have at least 3 ticks against each word (5 would guarantee a pretty foolproof imprint on your memory!)
- You can carry on these memory checks at odd moments during the day: just keep this book handy!
- Before you start on your next batch of about 30, always check the previous 30. You'll be surprised how the ticks mount up!
- When you come back to revise closer to your exam, repeat the process, adding a tick to each word you remember. Pay special attention to the words with fewer ticks!

You can also extend your vocabulary by taking a word and seeing how many related words you can find. For example, if you begin with *cocer* to cook, you could add *cocción* (process of) cooking, *cocido* stew, *cocina* kitchen, (skill of) cooking, cooker/stove, *cocinar* to cook, *cocinero/a* cook (person), etc. You could play this with a fellow student, each has to add a word. You can also do it with words associated by ideas: *cocina - gas - eléctrico - electricidad - luz - alumbrar* etc., or by opposites: *empezar-terminar; permitir-prohibir.*

And finally and most importantly: when you know these words, incorporate them into your work, whether it is written or spoken. If you don't use it you will lose it! *¡Suerte!*

Phil Turk

Acknowledgements

I would like to thank: Yvonne Chadwick and Mike Zollo for some useful comments and suggestions in the preparation of the material; Mercedes Catton, Antonio Moreno Carrascal and Virginia Vinuesa Benitez for reading the typescript and suggesting further additions and adjustments; my wife, Brenda, for her customary patience, encouragement and proof-reading.

Contents

Orders: please contact Bookpoint Ltd, 130 Milton Park, Abingdon, Oxon OX14 4SB. Telephone: (44) 01235 827720, Fax: (44) 01235 400454. Lines are open from 9.00–6.00, Monday to Saturday, with a 24 hour message answering service.

British Library Cataloguing in Publication Data
A catalogue entry for this title is available from the British Library

ISBN 0340 77165 8

First published 1991
Second edition 1996
Third edition 2000
Impression number   10   9   8   7   6   5   4
Year   2004 2003 2002

Typeset by Transet Limited, Coventry, England
Printed in Great Britain for Hodder and Stoughton Educational, a division of Hodder Headline Plc, 338 Euston Road, London NW1 3BH by Cox & Wyman Ltd, Reading, Berkshire.

Para empezar

Getting started

primero	first, firstly
segundo	second, secondly
tercero	third, thirdly, etc.
en primer/segundo/tercer lugar	in the first/second/third place
al principio	at first, at the beginning
de antemano	beforehand
primero tenemos que preguntarnos	first we have to ask ourselves
primero, los datos	first, the facts
ordenar los datos	to get the facts in order
despejar el terreno	to clear the ground
¿de qué se trata?	what is it all about?
resumir el tema/la cuestión	to summarise the issue
afrontar el tema/la situación	to face (up to) the issue/ situation
éste es un tema que ya lleva algunos años/meses apareciendo en los medios	this is a topic which has been in the media for some years/months now
es un tema que me tiene muy interesado/a (preocupado/a)	it's a topic/subject which interests (worries) me a great deal
será conveniente establecer los argumentos en pro y en contra	it will be useful to establish the arguments for and against
examinar más minuciosamente los argumentos	to examine the arguments in more detail

El desarrollo del argumento

Developing the argument

a primera vista	at first sight
a corto plazo	in the short term
a largo plazo	in the long term
a fin de cuentas	after all, when all is said and done
en esto	at this point/stage
asimismo	likewise
por consiguiente por consecuencia }	consequently, therefore

1

en principio	in principle
por otra parte	on the other hand, what's more
además	besides, moreover
además de lo dicho	in addition to what has been said
es más	moreover
debido a esto	owing/due to this
de hecho	in fact
dicho de otro modo	in other words
dicho eso	that said, having said that
no sólo... sino...	not only... but...
o sea...	or to put it another way..., or rather...
como ya se sabe	as we already know
es decir	that is to say, i.e.
en este contexto	in this context
por añadidura	in addition
a propósito	by the way
tanto... como...	both... and...
es decir	that is to say, i.e.
como resultado (de)	as a result (of)
resulta que...	it turns out that, the result is
esto explica por qué	this explains why
no me explico por qué...	I don't understand why...
así	thus
así es que	therefore
se trata de	it's a question of
el tropiezo	the stumbling block
la clave del problema	the key to the problem
la solución obvia	the obvious solution
hay que tomar medidas urgentes	urgent measures must be taken
una crisis a escala mundial	a crisis on a world scale
una situación inquietante	a worrying situation
la preocupación predominante	the main worry
la situación va empeorando	the situation is getting worse
la situación sigue mejorando	the situation continues to improve
teniendo en cuenta el hecho de que	bearing in mind the fact that
dado que	given that

Puntos de vista

por supuesto	of course
claro que (+ *clause*)	of course...
desde el punto de vista de...	from the point of view of...
desde mi punto de vista	from my point of view
a mi parecer ⎫	
a mi modo de ver ⎭	in my opinion
a mí me parece que... ⎫	
yo opino que... ⎭	*I* think that...
es de presumir que... ⎫	
según cabe presumir ⎭	presumably
por mi parte	for my part
estoy de acuerdo con los que...	I am in agreement with those who...
estoy persuadido/a de que (+ *indic*)	I am persuaded that...
no estoy persuadido/a de que (+ *subj*)	I am not persuaded that...
esto me lleva a pensar que...	this brings me to think that...
las cifras atestan que...	the figures prove that...
como ya se sabe	as is already known
que yo sepa	as far as I know
que se sepa	as far as is known
el problema que se plantea es...	the problem to be addressed/the problem that arises is...
en realidad	in fact, in reality
a pesar de esto	in spite of this
aparte de eso	apart from that
al contrario	on the contrary, on the other hand
visto así	seen like that
por un lado	on the one hand
por otro lado	on the other hand
de todos modos ⎫	
de todas maneras/formas ⎭	in any case, anyway
en lo que concierne ⎫	
en cuanto a ⎭	as for
en lugar de eso	instead of that
mientras que	whereas
no cabe duda de que...	there is no room for doubt that...
no se puede negar que...	there no denying that...
es cierto que...	it's certain that...
hay que tener en cuenta (que...)	you have to bear in mind (that...)

Points of view

C

hay que subrayar la importancia de...	you have to bear in mind the importance of...
más vale... que...	it's better to... than...
vale considerar...	it's worth considering...
según toda probabilidad	in all probability
nadie ignora que...	everybody knows that, nobody is unaware that...
no se puede menos de pensar que...	one cannot help thinking that...
rechazar un argumento	to reject an argument
condenar rotundamente	to condemn roundly
hacer la vista gorda (a)	to turn a blind eye (to)
el argumento no está bien fundado	the argument won't hold water
el argumento no tiene pies ni cabeza	the argument is all at sixes and sevens
el argumento carece de sentido	the argument lacks sense/meaning
el argumento carece de sustancia	the argument lacks substance
es una ilusión creer que...	we're kidding ourselves if we believe that...
pongamos el argumento patas arriba	let's stand the argument on its head
por si acaso	just in case
no hay manera de saber si...	there is no way of telling whether...
desgraciadamente ⎱ por desgracia ⎰	unfortunately
para colmo	to cap it all
eso sería locamente optimista	that would be wildly optimistic
y por si eso fuera poco	and as if that were not enough
yo que tú/usted	if I were you
no hay manera de saber si	there is no way of knowing whether
no estoy totalmente a favor de (+ *noun or inf*)	I'm not entirely in favour of
no estoy ni a favor ni en contra de (+ *noun or inf*)	I'm neither for nor against
tengo que confesarme en contra de (+ *noun or inf*)	I have to admit I am against
no es un opinión/actitud que comparta yo	it's not an opinion/attitude which I share
el punto flaco del argumento	the weak point of the argument
cualquiera que crea esto	anyone who believes this...
el argumento no tiene nada que ver con la realidad	the argument has nothing to do with reality
a juzgar por...	to judge by..., judging by...

en función de...	in proportion to..., according to (in that sense)...
en razón de...	by reason of..., because of..., due to...
hay quienes dicen que...	there are those who say that...
otros constatan que...	others maintain that...
según una encuesta	according to a survey/opinion poll
sondar las opiniones	to sound out opinions
la (gran) mayoría opina que...	the (vast) majority think that...
la gente piensa que...	people think that...
según se oye	according to what one hears
aunque quisiera pensar de otra manera	although I would like to think otherwise
la verdad lisa y llana es...	the plain truth of the matter is...
cualquiera es capaz de ver que...	anyone can see that...
tengo que confesarme partidario/a del/de la comentarista	I have to confess to being on the side of the commentator

Por ejemplo

For example

para ilustrar el problema	to illustrate the problem
vamos a abordar otro aspecto	let us tackle another aspect
con respecto a...	with regard to...
para considerar el asunto más detalladamente	in order to consider the matter in more detail
vamos a profundizar	let us think about it in greater depth
pongamos por caso lo de...	let us consider the matter of...

¿Cómo?

How?

extremadamente	extremely
totalmente	completely, utterly
principalmente	mainly, principally
tanto más	all the more so
hasta cierto punto	to a certain extent
¿hasta qué punto?	to what extent?
en cierto modo en cierta manera/forma	in a certain way
de ningún modo de ninguna manera	in no way
apenas	hardly
en ninguna circunstancia	in no circumstance(s)

5

simplemente ⎫	simply, purely
sencillamente ⎭	
puramente	simply, purely, merely
prácticamente	practically, nearly
parcialmente	partially, partly
igualmente	equally, to the same extent
efectivamente	actually, in fact
parecido a... ⎫	like..., similar to...
similar a... ⎭	
por la mayor parte	for the most part, mostly
a cambio de...	in exchange for...
sin más ni más	without further ado
se trata de saber cómo	it's a question of knowing how...

F ¿Cuándo?   When?

durante estos últimos años/meses	in the last few years/months
en el momento que...	at the moment when...
en aquel mismo momento	at that very moment
cuanto antes ⎫	as soon as possible
lo más pronto posible ⎭	

G ¿Por qué?   Why?

según los datos	according to the facts
eso explica por qué...	that explains why...
se trata de saber por qué	it's a question of knowing why
se debe tratar de descubrir por qué	we must try to find out why
puesto que... ⎫	since..., because...
ya que... ⎭	
por cualquier razón	for whatever reason
la razón principal	the main reason
la piedra clave	the keystone, the keynote

H ¡Lo útil que es la palabrita que!   That useful little word that!

I

A number of phrases with '*que*' meaning '*that*' are already included in the various sections of this chapter. Here are some more, looked at from the point of view of whether they are followed by the subjunctive or not. When the phrase states a fact, the following verb is in the indicative.

| **ejemplo**: la gente está consciente | people are conscious/aware that |
| de que hay muchos atracos | there are a lot of muggings |

el caso es que...	the fact is that...
otro factor es que...	another factor is that...
no se puede negar que...	it cannot be denied that...
no cabe duda de que...	there's no room for doubt that...
es de suponer que...	one presumes/supposes that....
debemos tener en cuenta que...	we have to bear in mind that...
si nos damos cuenta de que...	if we realise that...
resulta que...	the result is/it turns out that...
de ahí que...	that's the reason why...
el dilema es que...	the dilemma is that...
actualmente se calcula que...	at the moment it is estimated/ calculated that...
parece ser que...	it seems that...
claro que es verdad que...	of course it's true that...
lo cierto es que...	the sure thing is that...
en efecto yo diría que...	in fact I'd say that...
quiero dejar muy claro que...	I want to make it very clear that...
un 70% de los entrevistados opina que...	70% of those interviewed reckon that...
hay quienes afirman que...	there are those who maintain that...
menos mal que...	it's a good job that...

II

When the phrase makes a judgement and/or implies a purpose, the verb which follows is in the subjunctive*:

ejemplo: mi preferencia sería que no ocurriera*	my preference would be that it shouldn't happen
¿por qué tenemos que soportar que...?	why should we put up with the fact that...?
es intolerable/insoportable que...	it's intolerable that...
a mí me parece lógico que...	it seems logical/sensible to me that...
no me sorprende que...	I'm not surprised that...
todo esto justifica que...	all this justifies (the fact) that...
¿no parece significativo que...?	doesn't it seem significant that...?
a mí me resulta curioso que...	I find it extraordinary that...
esto explica que...	this explains why...
sería un milagro que...*	it would be a miracle if...
¿no sería mejor que...?*	wouldn't it be better if...?
no es porque...	it's not because....

7

me preocupa bastante que...	I'm somewhat worried that...
a mí no me importa que...	it's of no concern to me whether/that...
más vale que...	it's better/best that...
hay que asegurar que...	one has to ensure that...
si no fuera porque...	if it weren't for the fact that...
es de suma importancia que...	it is of extreme importance that...
¿por qué no exigimos todos que...?	why doesn't everyone demand that...?
es de lamentar que...	it is to be regretted that...
es una vergüenza nacional que...	it's a national disgrace that...
es una afrenta a la sociedad que...	it's an affront to society that...
es incluso más sorprendente que...	it's even more astonishing that...
parece inverosímil que...	it seems unlikely that...
parece mentira que...	it seems incredible that...
tiene que ser inconcebible que...	it has to be unthinkable that...
lo fundamental debe ser que...	the main thing should be that...
pongamos por caso que...	let us suppose that...

*Remember that the tense of the subjunctive will depend on the rules of tense sequence, and therefore phrases containing **sería**, which is conditional, would require the imperfect subjunctive.

Conclusiones

Conclusions

vuelvo a mi primera observación	I return to my first statement
ya hemos constatado que...	we have already stated that...
y volvemos al punto de partida	and we return to the starting point
en resumen	in brief, to sum up
por fin	finally, at last
en conclusión } para concluir }	in conclusion
teniendo en cuenta todos los puntos de vista	bearing in mind all points of view
aunque con ciertas dudas/reservas	although with certain doubts/reservations
la conclusión inevitable tiene que ser...	the inevitable conclusion has to be...
ojalá pudiera concluir diciendo que...	I wish I could conclude by saying that...
no hay otra conclusión que valga	there is no other valid conclusion

Las cualidades de tendencia positiva

Qualities tending to the positive

A

la cualidad	quality
la virtud	virtue
la preferencia	preference
el estado de ánimo	mood, frame of mind
relacionarse con la gente	to relate to/get on with people
llevarse bien con alguien	to get on well with someone
tener el don de...	to have the gift of...
tener el sentido del humor	to have a sense of humour
reflexionar antes de actuar	to think before acting
conservar la calma	to keep calm, keep one's cool
tomarse la vida como viene	to take life as it comes
actuar por instinto	to act instinctively
estar bien dotado de sentido común	to be well endowed with common sense
ser abierto/a	to be open, of an open disposition
ser alegre	to be happy, jolly (*i.e. that sort of person*)
ser amistoso/a } ser amigable	to be friendly
ser atento/a	to be thoughtful, kind
ser autosuficiente	to be self-sufficient
ser bondadoso/a	to be kind, generous
ser cariñoso/a	to be affectionate, loving, tender
cariño/a	darling, dear
ser cauto/a	to be cautious, wary
ser convencional	to be conventional
ser chistoso/a } ser agudo/a	to be funny, witty
ser diestro/a	to be skilful, clever
ser persistente	to be persistent
ser exigente	to be demanding
ser autoexigente	to expect a lot of oneself
ser extrovertido/a	to be an extrovert
ser feliz	to be happy (*by nature*)
la felicidad	happiness

ser honrado/a	to be honest
la honradez	honesty
ser imaginativo/a	to be imaginative
ser listo/a	to be *clever*
estar listo/a	to be *ready*
ser luchador/a	to be a fighter
ser maduro/a	to be mature
la madurez	maturity
ser optimista	to be an optimist (*by nature*)
estar optimista	to be optimistic (*about something*)
ser perceptivo/a	to be perceptive
ser perfeccionista	to be a perfectionist
ser risueño/a	to be cheerful, of a sunny disposition
ser sensible	to be sensitive
la sensibilidad	sensitivity
ser sincero/a	to be sincere
la sinceridad	sincerity
ser tolerante	to be tolerant
la tolerancia	tolerance

B

Los rasgos de tendencia negativa

Features tending to the negative

la obsesión	obsession
obsesionarse por...	to be obsessed with...
la fobia	phobia
no poder soportar	not to be able to put up with
el defecto	defect
estar en un constante estado de...	to be in a constant state of...
tener una tendencia a...	to have a tendency to...
odiar	to hate
el odio	hate, hatred
despreciar	to scorn, disdain
el desprecio	scorn, disdain
ver con malos ojos	to take a dim view of
sentirse algo inseguro/a	to feel a bit insecure
no ver más allá de las narices	not to see further than one's nose
tener mal genio	to be bad-tempered, of an evil disposition
volverse irritable	to get irritable
estar lleno de contradicciones	to be full of contradictions

hacer autobombo	to blow one's own trumpet
ser apático/a	to be apathetic
ser asqueroso/a	to be revolting, disgusting
ser brusco/a	to be abrupt, sharp, rude
ser canalla	to be a swine, a rotter
ser conflictivo/a ⎫ ser camorrista ⎭	to be argumentative, quarrelsome
ser chismoso/a	to be a gossip
los chismes	gossip, tittle-tattle
no ser honrado/a	to be dishonest
la falta de honradez	dishonesty
ser egoísta	to be selfish
ser emotivo/a	to be emotive, emotional
dejarse arrastrar por las emociones	to let oneself be ruled by one's emotions
ser encogido/a ⎫ ser tímido/a ⎭	to be timid, shy
ser envidioso/a	to be envious
ser engreído/a	to be conceited
ser fantasioso/a	to be conceited, stuck up
ser gruñón/gruñona	to be grumpy (*by nature*)
ser imbécil	to be an idiot
ser indeciso/a	to be indecisive (*disposition*)
estar indeciso/a	to be undecided (*at this moment*)
ser introvertido/a	to be an introvert
ser malévolo/a	to be malicious, spiteful
ser mezquino/a	to be mean, stingy
ser miedoso/a	to be timid, nervous
ser pesimista	to be a pessimist (*by nature*)
estar pesimista	to be pessimistic (*about something*)
ser posesivo/a	to be possessive
ser rebelde	to be unruly, rebellious
ser superficial	to be superficial
ser supersticioso	to be superstitious
ser terco/a	to be stubborn, obstinate
ser testarudo/a	to be stubborn, pigheaded
ser torpe	to be clumsy, awkward, dull, dim
ser vago/a	to be slack, lazy
ser vengativo/a	to be spiteful, vindictive
ser vengonzoso/a	to be shy, timid

11

A

Las relaciones en general

entablar amistades
el desarrollo de la personalidad
confiar en los amigos
compartir/guardar un secreto
llevarse bien/mal con...
tener una relación especial con...
respetar los sentimientos ajenos
tolerar a los demás
sentir alegría ante el bien ajeno
armar un follón
una relación heterosexual/
  homosexual
ser gay/lesbiana

Relationships in general

to strike up friendships
the development of the personality
to confide in, trust one's friends
to share/keep a secret
to get on well/badly with...
to have a special relationship with...
to respect other people's feelings
to tolerate others
to feel joy at others' wellbeing
to have a row, to kick up a fuss
a heterosexual/homosexual
  relationship
to be gay/lesbian

B

El amor y el matrimonio

ligar con un chico/una chica
el/la ligue
el novio/la novia

enamorarse
estar enamorado/a
el amor a primera vista ⎤
el flechazo   ⎦
llevar una relación seria
evolucionar una relación
sentirse atraído por...
estar chiflado/a por alguien
flirtear/coquetear con alguien
enrollarse con alguien
dar calabazas a alguien
prometerse (con)
soltero/a
estar casado/a
el noviazgo
están prometidos
la pareja

Love and marriage

to go out with/date a boy/girl
boy/girlfriend (*coll.*)
boy/girlfriend (*traditional*);
  bridegroom/bride
to fall in love
to be in love

love at first sight

to carry on a serious relationship
to evolve/work out a relationship
to feel attracted by...
to be infatuated with s.o.
to flirt with s.o.
to chat s.o. up
to jilt s.o.
to get engaged (to)
single
to be married
engagement
they are engaged
couple

prometer	to promise
el cariño	affection
cariñoso/a	affectionate
casarse (con)	to get married (to)
la boda	wedding
la madrina	bridesmaid
el padrino	best man
el anillo	ring
contraer matrimonio	to enter into matrimony
el voto	vow
hacer el amor	to make love
estar felizmente casados	to be happily married
sentir celos	to feel jealous
ayudarse uno a otro	to support each other
el apoyo mutuo	mutual support
la vida sexual	sex life

La familia y los niños / Family and children

los padres los progenitores	parents
estar embarazada	to be pregnant
quedar embarazada	to get pregnant
dejar embarazada a una mujer	to get a woman pregnant
parir	to give birth
el parto	birth, (in sense of) delivery
nacer	to be born
el/la bebé el nene/la nena	baby
la criatura	baby, small child
los gemelos	twins
tienen tres críos	they've got three kids
la nodriza	nurse, nanny
la niñera	childminder
la baja de maternidad/paternidad	maternity/paternity leave
el cochecito de niño	pram
la sillita de ruedas	pushchair
cambiar los pañales	to change nappies
el suegro/la suegra	father/mother-in-law
el cuñado/la cuñada	brother/sister-in-law
el protector/la protectora	guardian
el/la canguro	baby-sitter

hacer/estar de canguro	to baby-sit
el/la mayor	the elder/eldest
el/la menor	the youngest
el benjamín	the youngest son
el padrino	godfather
la madrina	godmother
los padrinos	godparents
el cumpleaños	birthday
cuando Pedro cumplió siete años	when Pedro was (– reached) seven years old
el santo	saint's day
el bautizo	christening, baptism
bautizar	to christen, baptise
se le puso Miguel	he was baptised Miguel
el nombre de pila	Christian name, first name
el jardín de infancia	kindergarten
la guardería (infantil)	nursery, crèche
la maternidad	maternity
amamantar	to suckle, breastfeed
dar el pecho	to breastfeed
la cuna	cradle
mecer	to rock
la infancia	infancy
los recuerdos de la niñez	childhood memories
la canción infantil	nursery rhyme
desde niño/a	from childhood
de niño/a	as a child
la paternidad	parenthood, fatherhood
criar una familia	to bring up a family
monopolizar el cariño de los padres	to monopolise parents' affection
en el seno de la familia	in the heart of/within the family
mostrar autoridad	to show authority
crear lazos de afecto	to create bonds of affection
evitar favoritismos	to avoid favouritism
crear un estrecho vínculo	to create a close bond
una familia unida	a close family
mimar a un niño	to spoil a child
el maltrato a los niños	child abuse

El divorcio

la tasa de divorcio
la orientación matrimonial
el consejero de orientación
  matrimonial
iniciar los procedimientos del
  divorcio
divorciarse
estar divorciado
solicitar un divorcio
el alejamiento
convivir
un proceso penoso
la ruptura matrimonial
ser incompatibles
cuando un matrimonio se deshace
la separación
separarse
perjudicar gravemente
hijos, bienes y posesiones
el padre soltero
la madre soltera
el custodio de los niños
el/la cónyuge
andar en relaciones con
la infidelidad
volver a casarse

La planificación familiar

la contracepción/anticoncepción
la píldora anticonceptiva
los métodos anticonceptivos

el anticonceptivo
el preservativo/condón
el control de la natalidad
un embarazo (no) deseado
interrumpir el embarazo
el feto
el ciclo menstrual

Divorce

the divorce rate
marriage guidance
marriage guidance counsellor

to initiate divorce proceedings

to get divorced
to be divorced
to apply for a divorce
estrangement
to live together
a painful process
marriage break-up
to be incompatible
when a marriage breaks up
separation
to become separated
to prejudice seriously
children, property and possessions
single father/parent (male)
single mother/parent (female)
custody of the children
spouse
to have an affair with
infidelity
to remarry

Family planning

contraception
contraceptive pill
contraceptive methods, birth
  control methods
contraceptive
condom
birth control
a wanted (unwanted) pregnancy
to terminate pregnancy
foetus
menstrual cycle

D

E

15

el aborto	abortion
abortar	to have an abortion/a miscarriage
fecundar	to fertilise
la hormona	hormone
concebir	to conceive
la fecundación in vitro	in vitro fertilisation
el niño probeta	test-tube baby
la inseminación artificial	artificial insemination
la madre portadora	surrogate mother

F

La tercera edad

Senior citizens

jubilarse	to retire
estar jubilado/a	to be retired
los jubilados	retired people
el/la pensionista	pensioner
la persona de la tercera edad	old age pensioner, senior citizen
la libreta de pensión	pension book
el plan de pensiones	pension scheme
la vida empieza a los 60 años	life begins at 60
el abono para la tercera edad	pensioners' travel pass
para las personas de 65 años o más } para los mayores de 65 años	for people of 65 and over
hacer lo que te dé la gana	to do as you please
el asilo de ancianos	old people's home
geriátrico	geriatric
estar postrado en cama	to be bed-ridden
el servicio de comidas a domicilio	meals on wheels
tener que depender de otros	to have to depend on others

 www.mujeractual.com/familia/index.html

El desafecto juvenil   Disaffection of young people   A

el movimiento juvenil	the youth movement
el desencanto	disenchantment, disillusion(ment)
el orden social	social order
el movimiento punk	the punk movement
el símbolo de frustraciones	symbol of frustration
la falta de oportunidades	lack of opportunities
asumir una actitud provocativa	to adopt a provocative attitude
sentirse perseguido/a y acosado/a	to feel persecuted and harassed
sentirse/estar marginado/a	to feel/be marginalised
la agresividad	aggressiveness
las luchas callejeras	street fights
lanzar improperios	to hurl abuse
el comportamiento	behaviour
comportarse	to behave
no se puede soportar este modo de comportarse	we can't put up with this sort of behaviour
bajo los efectos del alcohol o de la droga	under the influence of drink or drugs
la presión del grupo paritario	peer group pressure
el hurto	theft
el drogodelincuente	drug delinquent
la crispación	tension
los enfrentamientos	confrontations
no integrarse en el tejido social	to remain outside the social fabric
desperdiciar la juventud	to squander one's youth
vivir el presente	to live for the present
apurar el instante	to live for the moment
a mí no me extraña que haya tanta violencia	I'm not surprised that there's so much violence
hacerse el chulo	to act big/smart
la pandilla	gang
la tribu	tribe
la guerra tribal	tribal warfare
no soportar el aspecto de alguien	not to be able to stand someone's appearance
destrozarlo todo	to smash everything up

montar bronca	to cause a riot
necesitar una dosis de aventura	to need a dose of adventure
romper la aplastante rutina social	to break the soul-destroying daily routine
entonarse	to get high
la violencia futbolística	football violence
una orgía de violencia	an orgy of violence
desatar la violencia	to unleash violence
la bomba de humo	smoke bomb
el hincha ⎫ el forofo ⎭	fan, supporter (*football etc.*)
la prohibición de vender alcohol	prohibition of the sale of alcohol
mantener el orden	to keep order
un fenómeno creciente	a growing phenomenon
la protección policial	police protection
grupos organizados de fanáticos	organised groups of fanatics
el argot callejero	street slang

B	**Los problemas de hacerse adulto**	**Problems of growing up**

la permisividad paterna	parental permissiveness
estar en la edad de querer independizarse	to be of an age to want one's independence
le cuesta mucho concentrarse	he/she finds it difficult to concentrate
rebelarse contra la autoridad	to rebel against authority
montar un follón	to make a fuss
no se puede entender con su padre	he/she doesn't get on with his/her father
estar hecho un lío	to be all mixed up
deprimirse	to get depressed
sentirse deprimido/a	to feel depressed
cabrearse	to get mad, livid
tener problemas al relacionarse con la gente	to have problems relating to people
contar mentirillas	to tell lies, fibs
encontrarse inseguro/a	to feel insecure
superarse a sí mismo	to take oneself in hand, control oneself
la necesidad de ser uno mismo	the need to be oneself
el desarrollo de la personalidad	the development of the personality

no importa quién tiene razón	it doesn't matter who's right
reñir	to quarrel
llegar de madrugada	to come home in the small hours
ponerlo todo en tela de juicio	to question everything
de niño/a	as a child
ir creciendo	to be growing up
salirse con la suya	to get one's own way
mi madre es una antigualla	my mother is old-fashioned
mi padre es un chapado a la antigua	my father's an old fuddy-duddy
mis padres tienen las miras estrechas	my parents are narrow-minded
mis padres insisten en que yo (+ *subj*)	my parents insist that I...
mi padre me fastidia	my father gets on my nerves
mis padres no tienen prejuicios	my parents are open-minded
como si fuese lo único que importase	as if it were the only thing that mattered
compartir ideas	to share ideas
escuchar todos los días el mismo rollo	to hear the same old thing day after day
no es porque no lo intente	it isn't for want of trying
buscar cinco pies al gato	to make a lot of fuss over nothing, exaggerate
castigar	to punish
las reglillas	petty rules
cuestionar la autoridad	to question/challenge authority
soltar palabrotas	to swear, use bad language
mostrarse mal educado/a	to make a show of bad manners
mucho ruido y pocas nueces	a lot of fuss about nothing
hacer las paces	to make it up

La música pop

Pop music

la canción	song
grabar en disco	to record
la letra	lyrics, words (of a song)
el pinchadiscos	disc-jockey, DJ
la estrella de pop	pop star
la gira por Estados Unidos	US tour
el concierto	gig, concert
el festival pop	pop festival

C

las listas de éxitos	the charts
el disco número uno	number one hit
el sistema de amplificación	P.A. system
los amplificadores	loudspeakers, amplifiers
el teclado	keyboard
tocar la batería	to play the drums
los palillos	drumsticks
tocar la guitarra eléctrica	to play the electric guitar
el sintetizador	synthesiser
el/la solista	lead (*singer/player*)
doblar	to dub
las luces estroboscópicas	strobe lights
los focos	lights
los fans	fans

La moda — **Fashion**

el diseñador	designer
el modisto/la modista	fashion designer
la creación original	original creation
tener un buen aspecto	to look good
dar una buena imagen	to give a good image
la manera de vestirse	way of dressing
lucir un nuevo vestido	to wear/show off a new dress
la preocupación por vestir bien	the desire to be well-dressed
la caída de la chaqueta	the fall of a jacket
los vuelos de la falda	the spread/swirl of a skirt
saber elegir lo más elegante	to know how to choose the smartest (clothes, etc.)
saber cómo vestir	to know how to dress, have good dress sense
vestirse de una manera estrafalaria	to dress outlandishly
vestirse al estilo punk	to dress in punk style
lucir una cazadora de cuero negro	to sport/wear a black leather bomber jacket
los vaqueros rotos	ripped jeans

www.mtas.es/injuve/default.htm

La escolaridad

The school system

A

el centro docente	educational establishment
el centro	often used just to denote *school*
Educación Básica Obligatoria	compulsory basic education
Educación Primaria	primary education
Educación Secundaria Obligatoria	compulsory secondary education
el módulo	module
el colegio privado	private school
el instituto/colegio público	state school
el internado	boarding school
la academia	'crammer'
el parvulario	play school
un traslado de colegio	a change of school
el curso	school year
pasar de curso	to move up a year
la escolaridad	period of schooling
la asignatura	subject
la vuelta al cole/colegio	back to school
matricularse	to sign on, to enrol (*for a school*)
el rendimiento escolar	school performance
las clases particulares	private classes
los métodos de enseñanza	educational/teaching methods
el folleto de información	information booklet
un sistema adecuado a las capacidades y aptitudes del alumno	a system suited to the capabilities and aptitudes of the pupil
desarrollar su capacidad autocrítica	to develop one's capacity for self-appraisal
un método infalible	an infallible method
las asignaturas que presentan mayor dificultad	the subjects which present the greatest difficulty
las asignaturas que se pueden superar con más facilidad	the subjects which can be most easily mastered
el temario	syllabus
ser curroadicto/a	to be a workaholic
el alumno talentoso/la alumna talentosa	gifted pupil

estar bien motivado/a	to be well motivated
me falta la motivación	I lack motivation
me cuesta concentrarme	I have a job to concentrate
tener aptitud para los idiomas	to have a flair for languages
ser empollón/empollona	to be a swot
no vale el esfuerzo	it's not worth the effort
no soy muy bueno/a en ciencias	I'm not very good at science
¡ya caigo!	got it!
no caigo	I don't get it
devanarse los sesos	to rack one's brains
la capacidad de trabajo	capacity for work
tener la sed de conocimientos	to have a thirst for knowledge
hacer un mayor esfuerzo	to make a greater effort
abordar primero las asignaturas difíciles	to tackle the difficult subjects first
organizar el tiempo	to organise one's time
obtener resultados	to obtain results
conocer sus deficiencias	to know one's weaknesses
la capacidad de retener	the ability to retain knowledge
perder el hábito del estudio	to get out of the habit of studying
los problemas escolares	problems at school
el fracaso escolar	failure at school
fracasar	to fail, to be a failure (*in school*)
la falta de escolaridad	lack of schooling
las expectativas de los progenitores	parents' expectations
la sobreexigencia	over-expectation
flojear/ser flojo/a	to be weak
la escasa atención de los padres	lack of parental attention
la dislexia	dyslexia
sufrir retraso escolar	to fall behind in one's schooling
repetir curso	to repeat a year
faltar a clase	to skip lessons
la masificación	overcrowding
en las aulas	in the classrooms
las materias obligatorias	compulsory subjects
garantizar/mejorar la calidad en enseñanza	to guarantee/improve the quality of education
las instalaciones deportivas	sports facilities
los materiales trasnochados	out-of-date materials
la igualdad de oportunidades	equality of opportunities

ampliar la formación	to broaden one's education
mandar partes a casa	to send a report home
moldear las generaciones futuras	to shape future generations
la política educativa del Gobierno	Government education policy
la natalidad de los años noventa	the birth rate in the nineties
el gasto estatal en educación	state expenditure on education
proceder de las clases sociales más desfavorecidas	to come from the most disadvantaged social classes

Los profesores / Teachers

hacer oposiciones para profesor(a)	to apply for a teaching job
enseñar una asignatura	to teach a subject
dar clase a los alumnos	to teach pupils
el claustro	staff meeting
el catedrático/la catedrática	head of department/faculty
el agregado/la agregada	assistant teacher
el/la PNN (penene) = profesor(a) no numerario/a	probationary or lowest rank teacher
mantener la disciplina	to maintain discipline
el/la pedagogo/a	teacher, pedagogue
el/la profe	teacher (*coll.*)
los profesores reclaman su valoración en la sociedad	teachers demand to be appreciated in society
relacionarse con los alumnos	to relate to one's pupils
no tener favoritismos	not to have favourites
ser autoritario/a	to be authoritarian
ser capaz de motivar a los alumnos	to be capable of motivating pupils
poco exigente	undemanding, lax
relajado/a	relaxed, laid back
austero/a	austere
estricto/a	strict
fomentar la discusión	to encourage discussion
esforzarse en hacer las clases más agradables	to try to make classes more enjoyable
el castigo	punishment
castigar	to punish
reciclarse	to retrain

B

C Los exámenes

Examinations

la evaluación — assessment (*test held several times during the school year in Spanish schools*)

sacar buenas/malas notas — to get good/bad marks
sacar un sobresaliente — to get an 'excellent'
    un notable — a 'very good'
    un bien — a 'good'
    un suficiente — a 'satisfactory'
    un insuficiente — an 'unsatisfactory'
    un muy deficiente — a 'very poor'
aprobar un examen por los pelos — to scrape through an exam
suspender un examen — to fail an exam
aprobar por los pelos — to pass by the skin of one's teeth
la recuperación — retake
salir preparado para poder incorporarse al mercado de trabajo — to come out ready and able to be absorbed in the labour market
la chuleta — 'crib'

D La universidad

University

el sistema universitario — the university system
acceder a la enseñanza universitaria — to gain access to university education
ingresar en la universidad — to get into university
la solicitud de admisión — entry application
lograr títulos — to get qualifications
la selectividad — university entrance exams
el procedimiento de selección — selection procedure
cursar estudios universitarios — to follow a university course
la facultad universitaria — university faculty
el intercambio de conocimientos — exchange of knowledge
la libre circulación de las ideas — free circulation of ideas
una convalidación mutua de títulos — a mutually agreed validation of qualifications (*between countries*)

fomentar la discusión — to encourage discussion
las humanidades — arts, humanities
las ciencias — sciences
las tasas — tuition fees
conseguir una beca — to get a grant

el préstamo gubernamental	government loan
reembolsar un préstamo	to repay a loan
estar pelado/a	to be hard up
estar sin blanca	to be strapped for cash
una experiencia enriquecedora	an enriching experience
el enriquecimiento	enrichment
el desarrollo cultural/científico/ tecnológico	cultural/scientific/technological development
la licenciatura	degree
ser licenciado/a de derecho	to have a degree in law
la tesis doctoral	doctoral thesis
la fuga de cerebros	brain drain
las manifestaciones estudiantiles	student demonstrations
el líder estudiantil	student leader

www.comune.torino.it/~infogio/guida/espa_nat/4afr.htm
www.mec.es

La carrera	Career
ser ambicioso	to be ambitious
mi única ambición es hacerme...	my one ambition is to become a...
buscarse una carrera en el campo de las lenguas	to seek a career in the language field
le falta ambición	he/she has no ambition
apuntar alto	to aim high
un puesto de trabajo	a job
planificar su futuro	to plan one's future
poner las miras en un puesto alto	to set one's sites on a top job
sacar adelante la carrera	to foster one's career
andar en busca de empleo	to be on the lookout for a job
aspirar a periodista	to have aspirations as a journalist
prepararse para fontanero	to train as a plumber
seguir un curso de ingeniería	to follow a course in engineering
hacer un aprendizaje en carpintería	to do a carpentry apprenticeship
estudiar para abogado	to study to become a lawyer
promocionar la imagen	to promote one's image
soñar con hacerse estrella de cine	to dream of becoming a film star
el anuncio	advertisement
responder a un anuncio	to reply to an advert
se necesita fontanero	vacancy for a plumber
la agencia de colocaciones	employment agency
el INEM (Instituto Nacional de Empleo)	Ministry of Employment, (also equivalent of) government job centre
leer en las 'ofertas de trabajo'	to read in the 'Situations Vacant'
la formación	training
un trabajo muy solicitado	a much sought-after job
trabajar de camarero	to work as a waiter
la entrevista	interview
entrevistarse bien	to interview well
vestirse bien	to dress well
ser apto/a para el trabajo	to be suitable for the job

incorporarse al trabajo lo antes posible	to go out to work as soon as possible
conseguir un trabajo por enchufe	to get a job through connections, by pulling strings
estar bien enchufado/a	to have good connections
solicitar un puesto de trabajo	to apply for a job
hacer oposiciones	to seek a job by public competition (*in Spain*)
la hoja de solicitud	application form
escribir una carta de solicitud	to write a letter of application
el currículo	curriculum vitae, CV
los datos personales	personal data
los títulos académicos	academic qualifications
con licenciatura en ...	with a degree in ...
experiencia profesional	professional/work experience
tener el dominio del español	to speak good Spanish
las aficiones	interests
pedir informes/referencias	to ask for references
dar informes/referencias	to give references, act as referee
en respuesta a su anuncio publicado en...	in reply to your advertisement published in ...
tengo un año de experiencia en ...	I have a year's experience in ...
aunque no tengo experiencia en ...	although I have no experience in ...
me permito dirigirme a usted para (+ *inf*)	I am writing to you in order to ...
ofrecer mis servicios como	to offer my services as
el rechazo	rejection, refusal
me ofrecieron el trabajo	I was offered the job
me rechazaron	they turned me down
rechacé el puesto	I turned the job down
el potencial adquisitivo	earnings potential

El personal

Staff, personnel

el director general	managing director
el director de ventas	sales manager
el director de personal	personnel manager
los altos cargos	top people
el encargado	foreman
la plantilla	staff
la mano de obra	workforce
el obrero/la obrera	worker

B

el funcionario/la funcionaria	civil servant
el empleado/la empleada	employee
el empresario/la empresaria	manager/boss
el trabajador/la trabajadora	worker
el peón	unskilled worker
el aprendiz/la aprendiza	apprentice
el aprendizaje	apprenticeship
experimentado/a	experienced
generar empleo	to generate employment
cambiar de empleo	to change jobs
la satisfacción en el trabajo	job satisfaction
el estatus	status
el/la secretario/a de dirección	management secretary
un puesto de alta dirección	a senior management position
solicitar un puesto de trabajo	to apply for a job

C Las condiciones del trabajo — Working conditions

la empresa	firm, company
el mercado de trabajo	the labour market
un trabajo especializado	a specialised job
el peonaje	labouring
un trabajo de cuello blanco	a white-collar job
el sector de servicios	the service sector
la experiencia laboral	work experience
la banca	banking
el empleado/la empleada de banco	bank employee
la oficina central	head office
el sucursal	branch
la población obrera	the working population
el trabajo a pleno tiempo	full-time work
el trabajo a tiempo parcial	part-time work
el trabajo a destajo	piecework
el trabajo a tiempo flexible	flexi-time
el trabajo por turnos	shiftwork
trabajar horas extra	to work overtime
ser trabajador/a autónomo/a	to be self-employed
la rentabilidad	profitability
la productividad	productivity
la competencia	competition
la creación de empleo	creation of employment
contratar	to contract, take on

el pluriempleo	having more than one job
el contrato	contract
asalariado	waged, salaried, earning
el salario mínimo	minimum wage
el sueldo	pay, salary
cobrar	to earn
las normas de seguridad	safety regulations
la discriminación sexual	sex discrimination
la incorporación de la mujer en el trabajo	the involvement/acceptance of women at work
la igualdad de oportunidad	equality of opportunity
las posibilidades de promoción	promotion possibilities
sentirse a gusto en el trabajo	to feel happy/at home in one's work
la guardería	crèche

En el trabajo	**At work**
La correspondencia comercial	Business correspondence

Note: in business correspondence, if you are writing to and/or on behalf of your company, you tend to use the plural, if you know you are writing to a particular person representing that company, use the singular. Unless you are very well acquainted with your addressee(s) you will normally use *usted/ustedes.*

Muy señor mío	Dear Sir (person to person)
Muy señora mía	Dear Madam (person to person)
Muy señores nuestros	Dear Sirs (from firm to firm)
Estimado Sr. Ramírez	Dear Mr Ramírez
Estimada Sra. Blas	Dear Mrs Blas
acuso/acusamos recibo de su carta del 12 de abril	thank you for your letter of 12th April
con referencia a su pedido del 8 de mayo	with regard to your order of 8th May
en respuesta a su anuncio en *El Diario*	in reply to your advertisement in *El Diario*
tenemos el gusto de informarles que...	we have pleasure in informing you that...
hemos recibido una solicitud de información sobre ...	we have received a request for information about...
le(s) agradecería/agradeceríamos nos mandara...	I/we would be grateful if you would send us...

tenga(n) la bondad de comunicarnos su respuesta lo antes posible	please reply as soon as possible
tenga(n) la bondad de responder/ fax/correo electrónico por vuelta de correo	please reply/fax/e-mail by return of post
de acuerdo con sus instrucciones	in accordance with your instructions
adjunto encontrará(n)...	please find enclosed...
le/la saluda atentamente	yours faithfully (from one person)
les saludan atentamente	yours faithfully (from company)

NB if in doubt, you can just say *atentamente*!

remitente/rte.	sender (*on back of envelope*)
impresos	printed matter
certificado	registered (*mail*)
confidencial	confidential
telefonear/llamar por teléfono	to phone
la llamada telefónica/el telefonazo	phone call
¿me pone con la centralita?	can you put me through to the switchboard?
¿de parte de quién?	who's calling?
está(n) comunicando	the line is engaged
¿podría llamarme más tarde?	could he phone me later?
la máquina de escribir	typewriter
el procesador de textos	word processor
escribir un documento a máquina	to type a document
archivar	to file
el taquígrafo/la taquígrafa	shorthand writer
tomar taquigráficamente	to take down in shorthand
el fichero	filing cabinet

(You will find a further large range of vocabulary associated with communications and information technology on pp. 91-94 and business and finance on pp. 86-88).

E

Las relaciones laborales	**Labour relations**
el sindicato	trade union
el sindicalismo	trade unionism
el sindicalista	trade unionist
el enlace sindical	shop steward
la solidaridad de la clase obrera	working-class solidarity
el representante	representative

la tasa de inflación	the inflation rate
la reducción de la jornada de trabajo	reduction of the working day
exigir retribuciones mejores	to demand better remuneration
las vacaciones retribuidas/pagadas	paid holidays
el coste de la mano de obra	labour costs
el derecho a la huelga	the right to strike
ponerse en huelga ⎱ ir a la huelga ⎰	to go on strike
la comisión	committee
el convenio colectivo	collective agreement
la convocatoria	strike call
convocar manifestaciones	to call demonstrations
reivindicar	to claim, demand
la reivindicación	claim, demand
la huelga salvaje	wildcat strike
la huelga de solidaridad	sympathy strike
imponer un período de enfriamiento	to impose a cooling-off period
las negociaciones	negotiations
cuarenta horas semanales	forty hour week
despedir por razones disciplinarias	to dismiss, sack on disciplinary grounds
la flexibilización de horarios	flexitime
negociar	to negotiate
la subida de salario	salary/wage increase
las condiciones del trabajo	working conditions
yo creo que hay otras formas de protestar y conseguir lo que se pide	I think there are other ways of protesting and achieving one's demands
la huelga es el método más eficaz con el que cuenta la gente para que la escuchen	striking is the most effective way to get people to listen to you
no se consiguió nada con la huelga	the strike achieved nothing

El paro

Unemployment

F

el paro ⎱ el desempleo ⎰	unemployment
estar parado/a ⎱ estar desempleado/a ⎰	to be unemployed

31

el subsidio	benefit
el subsidio de paro	dole
incorporarse a las colas de los parados	to join the dole queues
despedir	to sack, fire, dismiss
despedir temporalmente	to lay off
la reducción de la plantilla	reduction in staff
reducir la plantilla sin despedir	to reduce staff by natural wastage
obligar a una persona a que se jubile anticipadamente	to force someone into early retirement
el paro a largo plazo	long-term unemployment
las cifras del paro	the unemployment figures
sentirse rechazado/a	to feel rejected
sentirse sin valor	to feel worthless
los resultados psicológicos de estar parado/a	the psychological results of being unemployed
ser una estadística	to be a statistic
reciclar	to retrain
el reciclaje	retraining
jubilarse	to retire
los costes salariales	wage costs
adaptarse a los cambios	to adapt to changes
acostumbrarse a los cambios tecnológicos	to get used to technological changes

www.contamicro.es/links/politica.htm
www.mujeractual.com/trabajo/index.html
www.mtas.es/mujer/servicio.htm

A

Los deportes de equipo	Team sports
	I
las actividades lúdicas	recreational activities
ser deportivo/a	to be keen on sport, a sportsman/woman
la temporada de fútbol	football season
la selección	team (*selection*)
la plantilla	'squad'
los delanteros	forwards
los defensores	defence
la junta directiva	management committee
el enfrentamiento	encounter, confrontation
la fase final del Campeonato	the final phase of the Championship
la derrota por el Barcelona	the defeat by Barcelona
derrotar	to defeat
lograr el primer gol	to achieve the first goal
los seleccionadores	the selectors
el liderazgo	leadership
permanecer imbatido	to remain unbeaten
hacer circular el balón	to pass the ball round
el entrenador	trainer
entrenarse	to train
sobre el terreno de juego	on the field of play
la quiniela (futbolística)	football pools
el boleto	pools form
la liga	league
la copa	cup
el drop	drop goal
transformar	to convert
el penalty	penalty
el árbitro	referee, umpire
las competiciones europeas	European competitions
el partido tendrá lugar	the match will take place
el torneo	tournament
la competición	competition
los deportes competitivos	competitive sports
el equipo rival	the rival team

el espíritu de rivalidad	rivalry, competitive spirit
el espíritu de equipo	team spirit
el campeonato mundial	world championship
marcar tres goles/un ensayo	to score three goals/a try
ganar cinco puntos	to win/score five points
¿cuál es el tanteo?	what's the score?
el Real Madrid batió al Barcelona de dos a uno	Real Madrid beat Barcelona 2–1
batir el récord	to beat the record
empatar con...	to draw with...
el resultado fue empate cero a cero	the result was a nil-nil draw
el/la vencedor/a	the winner
pasarse los sábados en el campo de golf	to spend one's Saturdays on the golf course
el corredor/la corredora	runner, competitor, athlete
los Juegos Olímpicos	Olympic Games
la Olimpiada	Olympiad
conseguir una medalla de oro/plata/bronce	to get a gold/silver/bronze medal
la ciudad anfitriona	host city
el estadio	stadium
las instalaciones deportivas	sports facilities
el polideportivo	sports centre/complex
las pruebas	trials
el abono de temporada	season ticket
coger la iniciativa	to take the initiative
jugar bien bajo presión	to play well under pressure

B **Los deportes individuales** **Individual sports**

el tenis	tennis
el golpe	shot
el revés	backhand
la volea	volley
el saque	service
la cancha de tenis	tennis court
ser campeón/campeona internacional sobre hielo	to be an international ice champion
el patinaje sobre hielo	ice skating
el patinaje artístico	figure skating
la pista de patinaje	skating rink

entusiasmarse por el esquí	to be mad on skiing
las pistas de esquí	ski slopes
dedicarse al ciclismo	to do a lot of cycling
la vuelta a Francia	Tour de France
la carrera	race
ir a la caza	to go hunting/shooting
las carreras de caballos	horse racing
el hipódromo	racecourse
apostar	to bet
jugarse el dinero	to gamble
el juego de azar	game of chance
los deportes con un alto componente de riesgo	high-risk sports
bucear	to skin-dive
el buceo	skin-diving
el vuelo libre	hang gliding
el ala delta	hang glider
el ultraligero	microlight
despegar	to take off
aterrizar	to land
la pista de aterrizaje	runway, landing strip
pertenecer a un club de deportes acuáticos	to belong to a water sports club
acceder a un cursillo de iniciación	to go on a beginner's course
ser amante del aire libre	to be fond of the fresh air
el traje isotérmico	wetsuit
costearse el equipo	to afford the equipment
los gastos de mantenimiento	maintenance costs

Juegos y pasatiempos de salón

Indoor games and pastimes

un pasatiempo terapéutico	a therapeutic pastime
dedicarse al coleccionismo	to go in for collecting
coleccionar sellos	to collect stamps
ampliar su colección	to expand one's collection
reunir las antigüedades	to assemble, collect together antiques
el afán de guardar	the urge to hoard things
atesorar	treasure
tener valor sentimental/como curiosidad	to have sentimental/curiosity value

C

ir haciéndose con objetos	to go on acquiring things
tener una auténtica pasión de coleccionista	to have a real passion for collecting
una obra de arte	a work of art
la tienda especializada	specialist shop
sacar fotos/fotografías	to take photos
revelar un rollo de película	to develop a roll of film
la ornitología	ornithology, bird watching
los juegos de salón	indoor games
¿te apetece una partida de ajedrez?	do you fancy a game of chess?
la tabla/pieza de ajedrez	chess board/piece
dar mate	to checkmate
salir de excursión	to go on a trip
no hacer nada en absoluto	to do nothing whatever
echarse una siestecita	to have forty winks/a snooze
no mover un dedo para ayudar en la cocina	not to lift a finger to help in the kitchen
quedarse pegado al televisor	to be glued to the television
pasarse los ratos libres escuchando discos compactos	to spend one's free time listening to CDs
asistir a una clase nocturna	to go to an evening class
empezar con el español	to take up Spanish

La comida y la bebida · Eating and drinking

el restaurante de cinco tenedores	'five fork' (– *luxury*) restaurant
tomarse unos pinchos/unas tapas	to have some 'tapas'
la cocina española	Spanish cooking
saborear	to savour, taste
saber a ajo	to taste of garlic
el menú gastronómico	gourmet menu
ser goloso/a	to have a sweet tooth
ser glotón/glotona	to be a glutton
ser cocinero/a experto/a	to be an expert cook
ofrecer un ambiente acogedor	to offer a friendly atmosphere
no es un restaurante cualquiera	it's not any old restaurant
se come bien	the food's good
la bodega	wine bar
la denominación de origen	mark of origin (*of wine*)
vino corriente/peleón	ordinary wine, 'plonk'
la juerga	binge

la fiesta	party
emborracharse	to get drunk
estar **borracho como una cuba**	to be as drunk as a lord
ser **borracho**	to be a drunkard
cogerse una borrachera	to go on a drinking bout
la resaca	hangover
abstenerse del alcohol	to be teetotal
las bebidas sin alcohol	non-alcoholic drinks
someter a la prueba del alcoholímetro	to breathalyse

www.sportsline.com/u/worldwide/spain/index.html
www.sportsline.com/u/worldwide/argentina/index.html
www.softguides.com/guia_madrid/comer/comer.html

La administración y los habitantes

Administration and inhabitants

el habitante	inhabitant
el ciudadano/la ciudadana	citizen
el madrileño/la madrileña	citizen of Madrid
el barcelonés/la barcelonesa	Barcelona
el sevillano/la sevillana	Seville
el ambiente	ambience, atmosphere
la capital administrativa	administrative capital
la capital económica	economic capital
el municipio	town
el Ayuntamiento	town hall, town council
el concejo	council
el concejal municipal	town councillor
la Diputación	*equivalent of* District Council
el presupuesto comunitario	the community budget

El tráfico y el transporte

Traffic and transport

el casco urbano	city centre
la(s) hora(s) punta	rush hour, peak time
el caos del tráfico	traffic chaos
el atasco	traffic hold-up
atascarse	to be held up
el tráfico rodado	wheeled traffic
el embotellamiento	traffic jam, bottleneck
agravar el problema del tráfico	to worsen the traffic problem
aprovechar los transportes públicos	to make use of public transport
el abono	travel card
el descuento	discount
el usuario de los autobuses	bus user
los autobuses van hasta los topes	the buses are packed
la peatonalización	pedestrianisation
crear más zonas peatonales	to create more pedestrian areas
el puente	bridge
el paso elevado	flyover
el paso subterráneo	underpass

la autopista elevada	elevated motorway
la autovía	dual carriageway
la glorieta	roundabout
aparcar	to park
el aparcamiento subterráneo	underground carpark
no se puede estacionar	you can't park
estacionamiento prohibido	parking prohibited
la multa	fine
multar	to fine
el/la guardia de tráfico	traffic policeman/woman, traffic warden
el tráfico es desesperante	the traffic is impossible
la carretera de circunvalación	ring road
la necesidad de más variantes	the need for more bypasses
el carril de bus	bus lane
el cruce de peatones	pedestrian crossing
el semáforo estaba en rojo	the traffic lights were red
la calle de dirección única	one way street
la desviación	diversion
calle cerrada por obras	roadworks – street closed
la grúa	crane (*to tow away cars*)
remolcar	to tow (away)
el cepo	wheelclamp
el ruido infernal	infernal noise
el humo de los tubos de escape	exhaust fumes
emitir gases nocivos	to emit noxious fumes
causar problemas respiratorios	to cause respiratory problems
el circulo vicioso	vicious circle
la remodelación del centro	redevelopment, restructuring of city centre
la vigilancia policial	police watch
una solución al tráfico de Madrid	a solution for the Madrid traffic
la polución	pollution
polucionar	to pollute
la contaminación	pollution
contaminar	to pollute, contaminate
hacer estragos con la salud	to wreak havoc with one's health
el viajero diario/la viajera diaria	commuter
viajar diariamente al trabajo	to commute to work
la pista para ciclistas	cycle track
volver a descubrir la bicicleta	to rediscover the bicycle

el lobby ciclista	the cycling lobby
la zona peatonal	pedestrian zone
la acera	pavement

C La vivienda y el trabajo

Where people live and work

la aglomeración	conurbation
la ciudad dormitorio	dormitory town
el rascacielos	skyscraper
el inmueble	block of flats
la agencia inmobiliaria	estate agent's
la fábrica	factory
la chabola	hovel, shanty
las condiciones de vivienda	living conditions
los sin hogar	the homeless
modernizar	to modernise
el chalé	detached house
el propietario/la propietaria	owner, proprietor
el inquilino/la inquilina	tenant
el barrio	district, suburb
en las afueras	on the outskirts
el casco urbano	city centre
la vecindad	neighbourhood
los vecinos	neighbours
la manzana	block (of houses/flats)
el almacén	store (shop or warehouse)
el centro comercial	shopping centre
la gran superficie	hypermarket
los grandes almacenes	department store(s)
el domicilio	address, home
una casa de alquiler	a rented house
alquilar un piso	to rent a flat
arrendar	to rent
deber el alquiler	to owe the rent
la urbanización	urban development
la planificación urbana	town planning
el piso piloto	show flat
el inmueble de lujo	block of luxury flats
con cocina amueblada	with fitted kitchen
la residencia secundaria	second home
el espacio verde	green space
el barrio desfavorecido	run-down district

la casucha	hovel
los cambios sociales	social changes
la vivienda	dwelling
la vivienda unifamiliar	one-family dwelling/unit
la hipoteca	mortgage
la revalorización del centro	redevelopment of the city centre
la zona industrial	industrial zone/park
el polígono industrial	industrial estate
el polígono residencial	residential development, estate
dar prioridad a la estética	to give priority to aesthetic considerations
el solar de construcción	building site

D

La seguridad ciudadana / **Public safety**

el alumbramiento público	street lighting
la farola	street light
la inseguridad ciudadana	citizens' feeling of insecurity
el atraco	assault, mugging
atracar	to assault, mug
los problemas de los barrios céntricos	inner city problems
un problema con pocas vías de solución	an almost insoluble problem
mendigar	to beg
el mendigo/la mendiga	beggar
la mendicidad	begging
dormir al descubierto	to sleep rough
el vagabundo	tramp
la depravación urbana	urban deprivation
los vigilantes	vigilantes
la autodefensa	self-defence
la vigilancia vecinal	neighbourhood watch
la policía de barrio	neighbourhood police

www.softguides.com/index_madrid.html

La vida rural

La tierra

The land

el terreno	plot
tener 20 hectáreas de terreno	to have 20 hectares of land
la parcela	small plot, strip of land
no se puede vivir de la tierra	you can't live off the land
la huerta	market garden
la finca	property, country estate
la granja	farm (*usually small, N. Spain*)
el cortijo	farm, estate (esp. *Andalucía*)
el minifundio	smallholding, small farm
el latifundio	large estate
el minifundista	smallholder
el latifundista	owner of large estate
el minifundismo/latifundismo	ownership corresponding to the above, often with reference to problems caused by the respective systems
el terrateniente ausente	absentee landlord
heredar una parcela	to inherit a plot
la reforma agraria	agrarian/land reform
convertirse en ciudad dormitorio	to become a dormitory town
integrarse en una cooperativa	to join/form a cooperative
depender de la agricultura	to depend on agriculture
el campesino	peasant, countryman

La agricultura

Agriculture

el agricultor	farmer
la zona agrícola	agricultural/farming area
el pueblo agrícola	farming village
cultivar patatas	to grow potatoes
el cultivo de naranjas	orange growing
el cultivador de aceitunas	olive grower
el aceitunero	olive picker
la recolección de la aceituna	olive gathering
los cultivos	crops

los productos	produce, crops
la cosecha	harvest, crop
la cosechadora	combine harvester
cosechar a máquina	to harvest by machine
la mecanización de la agricultura	mechanisation of agriculture
coger a mano	to pick by hand
segar	to reap
la siega	reaping
la vendimia	grape harvest
arar la tierra	to plough (up) the land
el arado	plough
el surco	furrow
germinar	to germinate
irrigar	to irrigate
regar	to water, irrigate
la acequia	irrigation channel
el desagüe	drain, outlet
los cereales	cereals
sembrar trigo	to sow wheat
el trigal	wheatfield
el maíz	maize
el maizal	maize field
las verduras	greens, vegetables
las hortalizas	vegetables, garden produce
la necesidad de modernizar la agricultura	the need to modernise agriculture
el programa de modernización agrícola	agricultural modernisation programme
el invernadero	greenhouse
cultivar bajo plástico	to grow under plastic
favorecer abonos químicos/ orgánicos	to favour chemical/organic fertiliser
los nitratos calan la tierra	nitrates soak into the soil
el estiércol	manure
la tierra baldía	sterile, waste land
dejar en barbecho	to leave fallow, set aside
el cultivo orgánico	organic farming
el ganado	stock, livestock
la ganadería	cattle, cattle raising
el ganadero	stockbreeder, cattle raiser
la feria de ganado	cattle fair

43

tener 50 reses	to have 50 head of cattle
el caballo	horse
la yegua	mare
el novillo	bullock, steer
el vaquero	herdsman, cowman
el rebaño de ovejas/cabras	flock of sheep/goats
el pastor	shepherd
la trashumancia	transhumance (*seasonal movement of cattle to new pastures*)
pastar las vacas	to graze cows
el prado	meadow, pasture
la industria lechera	dairy farming
el ganado lechero	dairy herd
ordeñar las vacas	to milk cows
el ordeño	milking
la cuota para la producción de la leche	milk (production) quota
los productos lácteos	dairy produce
el establo	cowshed
el corral	farmyard
la cría de cerdos	pig breeding
los piensos	fodder

C Vivir en el campo

Living in the country

I

respirar aire puro	to breathe pure air
disfrutar el paisaje	to enjoy the scenery
dejar atrás el bullicio de la ciudad	to leave behind the bustle of the city
aprovechar la paz y tranquilidad	to enjoy the peace and quiet
vivir en armonia con la naturaleza	to live in harmony with nature
buscarse una vida tranquila	to seek a quiet life
la gente tiene tiempo para hablar	people have time to talk
amanecer con el canto de los pájaros	to wake up to bird song
encontrar la casita de sus sueños en el campo	to find one's dream cottage in the country
aislarse en lo más hondo del campo	to cut oneself off in the depths of the countryside

II

la necesidad de mejorar la red de carreteras	the need to improve the road network
se ha reducido el número de trenes	the number of trains has been cut
se tarda bastante en llegar a la ciudad	it takes quite some time to get into town
por falta de transportes públicos	through the lack of public transport
vivir en un pueblo aislado	to live in a remote village
se llega por una carretera estrecha y tortuosa	you get to it along a narrow, winding road
llena de baches	full of potholes
en caso de emergencia	in emergency
no estás seguro/a de que tengas la mejor atención médica	you're not sure of getting the best medical attention
los chismes del pueblo	village gossip
el 'qué dirán?'	what the neighbours say
meter la nariz en las vidas ajenas	to poke one's nose into other people's business
el ambiente opresivo de la vida del pueblo	the oppressive atmosphere of village life
la falta de servicios	the lack of services
cortar el suministro de agua/ electricidad	to cut off water/electricity supplies

III

el éxodo rural	the rural exodus
la emigración	emigration, migration (*from place of origin, not necessarily to or from abroad*)
emigrar	to emigrate
los trabajadores extranjeros	foreign workforce
marcharse a América/Barcelona	to go off to America/Barcelona
la falta de trabajo y oportunidades	lack of work and opportunities
en la esperanza de ganar más fuera	in the hope of earning more elsewhere
cobrar más en el extranjero	to earn more abroad
buscar una mejora del nivel de vida	to look for an improvement in one's standard of living
desarraigarse	to uproot oneself

ser incapaz de adaptarse	to be unable to adapt
volver al lugar de origen	to return to where you came from

La caza y la pesca

Hunting, shooting and fishing

el coto de caza	game reserve
la pesca de la trucha	trout fishing
la caza del perdiz	partridge shooting
la caza del zorro	foxhunting
cazar el ciervo	to go stag hunting
el cazador/la cazadora	huntsman/woman
el cazador furtivo	poacher
el faisán	pheasant
la escopeta	shotgun
disparar a un conejo	to shoot at a rabbit
matar un conejo a tiros	to shoot a rabbit (*dead*)
estar en pro/a favor de la caza	to be for/in favour of hunting
los derechos de los animales	animal rights
el activista de derechos de animales	animal rights activist
el deporte en que se mata a un animal	blood sport
estar en contra de los deportes crueles	to be against cruel sports
abatir un ave	to shoot/bring down a bird
la perdigonada	lead shot
los perros (de caza)	hounds
despedazar la presa	to tear the quarry to pieces
hay que preguntarse si la caza es cruel o no lo es	you have to ask yourself whether hunting is cruel or not
la matanza selectiva de focas	seal culling
la caña de pesca	fishing rod
el anzuelo	hook
el cebo	bait
pasar horas a orillas del rio	to spend hours on the river bank

www. www.mapya.es

46

Los ferrocarriles

Railways

A

La RENFE (Red Nacional de los Ferrocarriles Españoles)	Spanish Railways
FEVE (Ferrocarriles Españoles de Via Estrecha)	company which runs Spanish narrow gauge lines
el AVE (Alta Velocidad Española)	Spanish high-speed train
la red española de ferrocarriles	the Spanish railway network
el ancho de vía internacional	the international gauge
el tren de alta velocidad	high-speed train
la locomotora de gran potencia	high-powered locomotive
una velocidad superior a 200 kilómetros por hora	a speed above 200 km per hour
el transporte de mercancías	freight transport
modernizar el sistema	to modernise the system
ampliar la red	to extend the network
construir nuevas líneas	to build new lines
eliminar las líneas no rentables	to close down unprofitable lines
incrementar la inversión	to increase investment
reducir las tarifas	to reduce fares
quitar los trenes	to cut train services
el único medio de transporte público	the only means of public transport
es cuestión de rentabilidad	it's a question of profitability
conseguir un mayor número de pasajeros (de mercancías) en los trenes	to attract more passengers (goods) to rail
tener trenes eficaces y competitivos	to have an efficient and competitive train service

Las carreteras

Roads

B

mejorar el servicio de autobuses	to improve the bus service
mejorar el horario	to improve the timetable
a intervalos regulares	at regular intervals
los autobuses siempre van atestados	the buses are always full up
la línea de autobús	bus route
el transporte pasajero rápido	rapid passenger transport

el abono de transportes semanal/ mensual	weekly/monthly travel card
reintroducir los tranvías eléctricos	to reintroduce electric trams
la autopista	motorway
la autovía	dual carriageway
la carretera de peaje	toll road
el MOPU (Ministerio de obras públicas)	Ministry of Transport
el desplazamiento	movement (*from one place to another*)
desplazarse	to travel, move about
el tráfico de largo recorrido	long-distance traffic
la calzada	roadway
planificar la red de carreteras	to plan the road network
el programa de construcción de carreteras	road building programme
abrir un nuevo tramo	to open a new section (of road)
cometer un atropello ecológico	to commit an ecological outrage
evitar daño médioambiental	to avoid environmental damage
el coste medioambiental	the environmental cost
la infraestructura	infrastructure
el volumen de tráfico	volume of traffic
la seguridad	safety
el cruce peligroso	dangerous junction
el 'punto negro'	'black spot'
el cruce	crossroads/junction
el factor más importante en la planificación de las carreteras	the most important factor in road planning
la falta de dinero para pagar la infraestructura	the lack of money to pay for the infrastructure
la velocidad excesiva	excessive speed
incrementar los impuestos sobre la gasolina	to increase tax on petrol

C Los transportes aéreos — Air transport

la línea aérea	airline
el vuelo chárter	charter flight
el vuelo regular	scheduled flight
la seguridad aérea	air safety, safety in the air
el registro de equipaje	baggage search

radiografiar	to X-ray
facturar el equipaje	to check in
la franquicia de equipaje	baggage allowance
el jumbo	jumbo jet
el retraso	delay
el desfase	jet lag
la diferencia de horario	time difference
estrellarse con la pérdida de 300 vidas	to crash with the loss of 300 lives
el siniestro	disaster
la catástrofe	catastrophe, disaster
desplomarse del cielo	to fall out of the sky
atribuirse a un fallo humano	to be attributed to human error
el fallo mecánico	mechanical fault

Los transportes por agua — **Water transport**

el ferry	(car) ferry
el muelle	quay
la hidroala	hydrofoil
el aerodeslizador	hovercraft
el petrolero	oil tanker
el transatlántico	liner
el buque de carga	freighter
el buque salvavidas	lifeboat
los canales del interior	inland waterways
el Canal de la Mancha	English Channel
el Golfo de Vizcaya	Bay of Biscay
el (Mar) Mediterráneo	Mediterranean (Sea)
el Estrecho de Gibraltar	Strait of Gibraltar
la travesía	crossing
hacer un crucero	to go on a cruise
marearse	to get seasick
naufragar	to be shipwrecked
ahogarse	to be drowned
hundirse	to sink
el rescate marítimo	sea rescue
el puesto de guardacostas	coastguard station
se tarda más	it takes longer

D

El transporte particular

Private transport

el aparcamiento para turismos	parking for private cars
el aparcamiento subterráneo	underground car park
el parquímetro	parking meter
la multa de aparcamiento	parking ticket/fine
el permiso de conducir	driving licence
acelerar la marcha	to step on the gas
el Código de la circulación	Highway Code
adelantar	to overtake
la velocidad máxima	maximum speed
¡a más de 50 semáforo en rojo!	if you do more than 50kph the light will turn red!
la zona de velocidad controlada por radar	speed trap
ponerle una multa a alguien	to fine somebody
en el acto	on the spot
atropellar	to knock over, run over
tener un encontronazo	to have a collision
estrellarse contra	to crash into
chocar de frente	to crash head-on
patinar	to skid
el lesionado/la lesionada	casualty
tener una avería	to break down
estar averiado	to be broken down
hacer autostop/ir en autostop	to hitch-hike
el/la autostopista	hitch-hiker
compartir el coche	to 'car-share'
ofrecer llevarle a alguien	to offer someone a lift
prescindir del coche	to do without the car
dejar el coche en el garaje	to leave the car in the garage
un coche de alto consumo de gasolina	'gas guzzler'
incrementar el impuesto sobre el combustible	to increase the duty on fuel

El turismo

Tourism

España está a tope de turistas	Spain is bursting with tourists
se espera recibir a cuarenta millones de visitantes	forty million visitors are expected
las playas están a rebosar	the beaches are overflowing

las zonas costeras	the coastal areas
no se puede encontrar ni hotel ni apartamento	you can't find a hotel or an apartment
los excursionistas	day-trippers
las previsiones para este año	the forecast for this year
la localización geográfica	geographical situation
estar a dos horas de vuelo de Londres	to be two hours' flight from London
llegar en el ferry desde Plymouth	to arrive on the Plymouth ferry
España es un país turísticamente muy organizado	Spain is a well-organised tourist destination
la relación precio-calidad	the price-quality ratio
el turismo de masas	mass tourism
el turismo de calidad	quality tourism
el turismo alternativo	alternative tourism
la industria hotelera	hotel industry
la estacionalidad	seasonal variation (*of demand*)
la infrautilización de la capacidad hotelera	the under-use of hotel accommodation/capacity
un centro turístico de primera categoría	a first-class tourist centre
desembolsar importantes sumas de dinero	to lay out considerable sums of money
gastarse un dineral	to spend a small fortune
desarrollar el interior	to develop inland areas
dirigirse tierra adentro	to go inland
una ciudad monumental	a historic town
para el turista perspicaz	for the discerning tourist
el tour operador	tour operator
el paquete	package
el viaje con todo incluido	package tour
el coste del alojamiento	cost of accommodation
la doble reserva	double booking
el libro de reclamaciones	complaints book
formular una reclamación	to lodge/make a complaint
una habitación con vistas al mar	a room with a sea view
la habitación da a un solar	the room looks onto a building site
el gamberrismo	loutishness, yobbishness
las invasiones de gamberros extranjeros	invasion of foreign yobs

G

Las vacaciones	Holidays
olvidar la rutina diaria	to forget the daily routine
descansar del ajetreo cotidiano	to relax from the daily grind
el crucero	cruise
para todos los gustos	for all tastes
disfrutar de unas buenas vacaciones	to enjoy a good holiday
a un precio	at a price
costearse unas vacaciones	to afford a holiday
al alcance de cualquiera	within anyone's reach
no supone un gran desembolso	it doesn't involve a large outlay
escoger un sitio marchoso	to choose a trendy place
la movida nocturna	the night life
buscarse unos días de paz y tranquilidad	to seek a few days' peace and quiet
nada más relajante que...	there's nothing more relaxing than...
tomar el sol en la playa	to sunbathe on the beach
broncearse	to get a suntan
un sitio alejado del ruido de las ciudades	a place far from the city noise
pasarlo bomba	to have a whale of a time
estar a sus anchas	to be at one's ease

www.viajes-venezuela.com/19991226-0109.htm
www.renfe.es/viajes/index.html
www.spainter.com/marina/index.html
www.mir.es/trafico/traf.htm

La televisión

Television

I

el televisor	television (*set*)
la tele	TV, telly
poner/quitar la tele	to turn the telly on/off
la programación	programme times
el monopolio público	public monopoly
el monopolio oficial televisivo	the official television monopoly
la empresa privada	private company
el canal / la cadena	channel
una gama amplia de canales	a wide range of channels
el espacio	(programme) slot
el concurso	competition
el/la telespectador/a	viewer, television watcher
la pantalla chica	the small screen
el receptor	receiver
la 'caja tonta'	'goggle box'
el mando a distancia	remote control
la televisión por cable	cable television
la emisora	broadcasting station, transmitter
la televisión por satélite	satellite television
la (antena) parabólica	satellite dish
la telenovela	soap opera
el dibujo animado	cartoon
las actualidades	current affairs
el telediario	news programme
por enésima vez	for the umpteenth time
una gama de programas	a range of programmes
el influjo sobre los valores morales	the influence on moral values
los anuncios	advertisements
una fuerza social destructora	a destructive social force
la violencia televisiva	television violence
una gran ayuda educativa	a great educational aid

II

adaptar su propio horario al de la tele	to adapt one's own timetable to the TV
ejercer control sobre la selección de los programas	to exercise control over the choice of programmes
avivar la imaginación	to sharpen the imagination
proporcionar cultura	to propagate culture
producir un efecto hipnótico	to have a hypnotic effect
producir la pérdida de capacidad creativa	to bring about a loss of creativity
coartar la agilidad mental	to stultify mental agility
perjudicar el desarrollo del niño	to prejudice a child's development
dosificar el tiempo ante el televisor	to measure/ration time spent in front of the TV

III

el vídeo	video (*all senses*)
la película de vídeo	videofilm
grabar en vídeo	to video
el videocasete	video cassette
la videograbadoa	video recorder
el videofilm de terror	video nasty
la pornografía	pornography
la porno	porn
el vídeo porno	porn video
pornográfico	pornographic

B   La prensa

The press

el diario	daily paper
la revista semanal/mensual	weekly/monthly magazine
la circulación	circulation
el/la periodista	journalist
el reportero/la reportera	reporter
dar una rueda de prensa	to give a press conference
defender la libertad de la prensa	to defend the freedom of the press
la censura de la época franquista	the censorship of the Franco years
luchar contra el censor	to fight against the censor
aparecer en las columnas del periódico	to appear in the newspaper columns
los titulares proclaman...	the headlines proclaim...
tener prejuicio contra...	to be biased against...

ser partidario de...	to be biased in favour of...
tener propensión a...	to be biased towards...
un juicio parcial	biased judgement
apoyar una opinión política	to support a political opinion
el redactor/la redactora	editor
redactar un periódico	to edit a newspaper
el artículo de fondo	editorial article
la prensa sensacionalista	gutter press
la consultora sentimental	'agony aunt'
el triunfo	triumph, 'scoop'
invadir la intimidad de alguien	to invade somebody's privacy
se meten en todos sitios con sus cámaras	they get in everywhere with their cameras
la censura	censorship
demandar a alguien por difamación	to sue somebody for libel
la revista del corazón	glossy, romantic magazine (e.g. *¡Hola!*)
el 'tabloide'	tabloid

La publicidad

Advertising

la industria publicitaria	advertising industry
la agencia publicitaria	advertising agency
la cartelera	hoarding
el cartel (publicitario)	(advertising) poster
el anuncio	advertisement
los pequeños anuncios	small ads
promocionar	to promote
el mensaje	message
la consignación de publicidad	advertising budget
llamativo	appealing, eye-catching
el consumidor/la consumidora	consumer
la sociedad consumista	consumer society
llamar a nuestros instintos más bajos	to appeal to our baser instincts
la interrupción constante de los programas	constant interruption of programmes
la actitud sexista de los anunciantes	the sexist attitude of the advertisers
el poder adquisitivo	purchasing power
hacer impacto	to make an impact
dirigirse al consumidor joven	to target the young consumer
manipular	to manipulate

A

La medicina preventiva	**Preventive medicine**
promocionar la salud	to promote health
el medicamento	medicine (*which you take*)
estar en buena forma/condición	to be in good physical shape
mantenerse en forma física	to keep fit
la función vital	vital function
preocuparse por la salud	to worry about one's health
el ambulatorio	outpatient dept., health service hospital
pasar una revisión médica	to have a medical examination
el chequeo	check-up
detectar a tiempo	to detect in time
atajar la aparición de enfermedades	to forestall the onset of disease
un diagnóstico precoz de determinadas dolencias	early diagnosis of certain illnesses
comprobarse el nivel del colesterol	to check one's cholesterol level
la vacuna	vaccine
vacunarse contra la fiebre del heno	to be vaccinated against hay fever
la exploración (médica)	(medical) investigation, check-up
diagnosticar	to diagnose
poner de manifiesto	to bring to light
tener propensión especial a un determinado mal	to be particularly susceptible to a specific complaint
los signos clínicos	the clinical signs
más vale prevenir que curar	prevention is better than cure
envejecer	to age
darse un respiro	to give oneself a break
el ritmo biológico	biological rhythm
la educación sanitaria	health education
autodiagnosticarse	to make a self-diagnosis
el autodiagnóstico	self-diagnosis
la higiene	hygiene
llevar un modo de vida sano	to lead a healthy life
la necesidad del ejercicio regular	the need for regular exercise
una dieta sana	a healthy diet

Los síntomas y las enfermedades

Symptoms and illness

I

el microbio	microbe, 'bug'
la epidemia	epidemic
la alergia	allergy
alérgico/a	allergic
tener alergia a	to be allergic to
el síndrome de alergia total	total allergy syndrome
el agotamiento	exhaustion
el estrés/la tensión	stress
estar hecho polvo	to feel a wreck
no poder más	to be at the end of one's tether
desvelarse	to be unable to sleep, to lie awake
el cansancio físico y mental	physical and mental tiredness
echar mano a un medicamento	to reach for the medicine
evitar contagios	to avoid infection
contagiarse (de)	to become infected (with), to catch
el trastorno	upset, trouble
el período de incubación	incubation period
pasar desapercibido	to go unnoticed, undetected
padecer una dolencia	to suffer from an illness
el minusválido/la minusválida	disabled person
la minusvalía	disability
tener una lesión grave	to have a serious injury
las enfermedades invernales	coughs and colds, winter illnesses
caer enfermo/a	to fall ill
la diabetes	diabetes
la pulmonía	pneumonia
el SIDA	AIDS
transmitir por los fluidos corporales	to transmit via body fluids
ser seropositivo	to be HIV positive
el cáncer del pulmón	lung cancer
el infarto	heart attack
las enfermedades cardíacas	heart disease
las viruelas	smallpox
el paludismo	malaria
la amigdalitis	tonsilitis
la bronquitis crónica	chronic bronchitis*

la tuberculosis   tuberculosis*

* Most diseases which end in *–is* English are identical in Spanish except for
adaptation to the Spanish spelling system (**bronquitis**). They are always feminine.

II

la depresión   depression
deprimirse   to become depressed
la salud mental   mental health
la enfermedad mental   mental illness
estar acomplejado   to have a complex
recibir tratamiento psiquiátrico   to undergo psychiatric treatment
el/la psiquiatra   psychiatrist
los nervios se me disparan   my nerves are at breaking point
tener los nervios destrozados   to be a nervous wreck
el colapso nervioso   nervous breakdown
padecer de los nervios   to suffer from one's nerves

C Los remedios y el tratamiento   Remedies and treatment

las contraindicaciones   contraindications
los efectos secundarios   side-effects
el somnífero   sleeping tablet
el tranquilizante   tranquilliser
el analgésico   analgesic, pain-killer
la terapia   therapy
seguir un curso de fisioterapia   to follow a course of physiotherapy
operarse   to have an operation
el equipo médico de urgencia   emergency medical team
despejarse la nariz   to clear one's nose
sonarse las narices   to blow one's nose
un descongestivo nasal   a nasal decongestant
las más avanzadas técnicas en   the most advanced surgical
   cirurgía   techniques
el tratamiento curativo   curative treatment
la anestesia general/local   general/local anaesthetic
el trasplante de riñón   kidney transplant
el/la donante de órganos/riñón   organ/kidney donor
rechazar el órgano trasplantado   to reject the transplant
trasplantar   to transplant
responder al tratamiento   to respond to treatment
la hormona   hormone

¡que te mejores pronto!	get well soon!
romper un círculo vicioso	to break a vicious circle
hospitalizar	to hospitalise, put into hospital
pasar un rato en el hospital	to spend a while in hospital
se vende sólo con receta	obtainable only on prescription
recetar una droga	to prescribe a drug
la píldora	pill
el comprimido	tablet
curar	to cure
la transfusión de sangre	blood transfusion
el ambulatorio	outpatient dept., health service hospital
la longevidad	life expectancy
la natalidad	birth rate
la mortalidad	death rate

El tabaco y el alcohol

Tobacco and alcohol

D

fumar en pipa	to smoke a pipe (*as opposed to cigarettes*)
fumarse una pipa	to smoke a pipe (– *a pipeful*)
dejar de fumar	to give up smoking
inhalar	to inhale
cigarrillos con menos nicotina y alquitrán	cigarettes with reduced nicotine and tar
en caso de que te resulte imposible abandonar el cigarrillo	in the event of your being unable to give up cigarettes
perjudicar seriamente la salud	to seriously affect one's health
destrozarse los pulmones	to wreck one's lungs
ingerir en pequeñas dosis	to take in small doses
el excesivo consumo de alcohol	excessive alcohol consumption
beber alcohol en ayunas	to drink alcohol on an empty stomach
afecta a todo el organismo	it affects the whole system
los trastornos cardiocirculatorios	cardiovascular problems
la intoxicación aguda	acute intoxication
la borrachera	drunken state, binge
la capacidad de reflejos	reflex capacity
el nivel de alcohol en la sangre	blood-alcohol level
la resaca	hangover
someter a la prueba del alcoholímetro	to breathalyse

E

La droga	Drugs
el estupefaciente	narcotic
el depresor	depressant
los barbitúricos	barbiturates
la droga dura/blanda	hard/soft drugs
el drogadicto / el toxicómano	drug addict
la drogadicción	drug addiction
la toxicomanía galopante	accelerating drug addiction
la drogodependencia	drug dependency
el/la drogodependiente	person dependent on drugs
el/la drogodelincuente	drugs delinquent
la cocaína	cocaine
la 'coca'	cocaine (*not* Coca-cola)
el cocainómano	cocaine addict
la heroína	heroin
el heroinómano	heroin addict
el narcotráfico	drugs traffic
el narcotraficante	drug trafficker
el camello	drug pusher (*coll.*)
el chocolate	'dope', cannabis
el porro	joint, cannabis cigarette
penalizar el consumo de drogas en lugares públicos	to make the consumption of drugs in public places illegal
la legalización parcial de las drogas	the partial legalisation of drugs
esnifar	to sniff
la jeringuilla	syringe
inyectarse	to inject (oneself)
pincharse	to 'shoot up' (*coll.*)
costearse un vicio	to afford a vice
drogarse	to take drugs
doparse	to take dope
probar una droga	to try (out) a drug
el esnifamiento de disolvente	solvent abuse, glue-sniffing
estar totalmente en contra de la droga	to be totally against drugs
un programa de reinserción social	a programme of social rehabilitation
un programa de desintoxicación	a detoxification programme
el síndrome de abstinencia	withdrawal symptoms
tener el mono	to go 'cold turkey'
estar rabiando por un pinchazo	to be craving for a fix
la dosis fatal	fatal dose

El régimen | Diet

El régimen	Diet
el régimen } la dieta }	diet
el aporte justo de calorías	the right number of calories
los ingredientes calóricos	high-calorie ingredients
comer compulsivamente	to be a compulsive eater
quemar las materias grasas	to burn off fat
la obesidad	obesity
obeso	obese
el peso	weight
pesar demasiado	to be overweight
tener una obsesión por adelgazar	to have a slimming obsession
adelgazar cinco kilos	to lose five kilos
quitarse dos kilos	to take off two kilos
la anorexia nerviosa	anorexia nervosa
engordar	to put on weight
engordar ocho kilos	to put on eight kilos
tener doce kilos de más	to be twelve kilos overweight
esos kilos de más	that extra weight
una nutrición equilibrada	a balanced intake/diet
el pan integral	wholemeal bread
la fibra	fibre
las calorías	calories
la energía	energy
la miel es un alimento muy energético	honey is a food high in energy
cuidarse la línea	to watch one's figure
los 'michelines'	'spare tyre'
la materia grasa	fatty substances, fat
sentir hambre	to feel hungry

www.fitness-point.com
www.mujeractual.com/dietas
www.ocioweb.com/vaixell/salut/nutricion/dietas.htm

La guerra y la paz

13

A

La guerra en general	War in general
declarar la guerra	to declare war
emprender la guerra	to go to war
estar en guerra	to be at war
la guerra de nervios	war of nerves
la guerra fría	the cold war
cuando estalló la guerra entre...	when war broke out between...
en los años de la posguerra	in the post-war years
ganar	to win
derrotar	to defeat
vencer	to beat
invadir	to invade
la invasión	invasion
el ultimátum	ultimatum
aplastar las fuerzas enemigas	to crush the enemy forces
el botín	booty, spoils
la máquina de guerra	war machine
la agresión armada	armed agression
una fuerza potente	a powerful force
provocar una crisis	to provoke a crisis
las sanciones internacionales	international sanctions
la pérdida de vidas humanas	the loss of human life
las superpotencias	superpowers
atacar	to attack
el ataque	attack
si la situación se agrava	if the situation worsens
desatar una guerra	to unleash a war
el Ministerio de Defensa	Ministry of Defence
defender	to defend
la batalla	battle
la amenaza nuclear	the nuclear threat
prepararse para la confrontación/ el enfrentamiento	to prepare for confrontation
la jerarquía militar	military hierarchy
recibir órdenes	to receive orders
la Cruz Roja	Red Cross
el armamento nuclear	nuclear armament

el sistema de misiles	missile system
una guerra sangrienta	a bloody war
disparar	to fire (*a gun*)
la guerra química	chemical warfare
las armas químicas	chemical weapons
la guerra biológica	biological warfare
la guerra de las galaxias	star wars
la guerra de trinchera	trench warfare
el aliado	ally
una potencia aliada	an allied power
incapacitar	to incapacitate
lesionar	to wound, injure
el holocausto nuclear	nuclear holocaust

Las fuerzas armadas y el material bélico — The armed forces and military equipment · B

el ejército	army
las tropas	troops
la flota	fleet
la armada	navy
las fuerzas aéreas	air force
el portaaviones	aircraft carrier
el avión de caza	fighter plane
el bombardero	bomber
el radar	radar
las tropas aerotransportadas	airborne troops
el destructor	destroyer
la fragata	frigate
el buque de guerra	warship
el tanque	tank
el dragaminas	minesweeper
el coche blindado	armoured car
la bomba	bomb
el cohete	rocket
el obús	shell
el gas nervioso	nerve gas

El servicio militar — Military service · C

la mili	military service (*coll.*)
la prórroga	deferment (*of service*)

el objector de conciencia	conscientious objector
ser considerado no apto para la mili	to be considered unsuitable for military service
el voluntario	volunteer
el recluta	recruit
el desertor	deserter
eliminar el servicio militar obligatorio	to abolish compulsory military service
hacer voluntario el servicio militar	to make military service voluntary
la disciplina resulta dura	discipline is hard
estar a favor de un ejército profesional	to favour a professional army
hacer todo lo posible para evitar la mili	to do everything possible to avoid call-up

D **La paz**   **Peace**

mantener la paz	to keep the peace
hacer las paces (con)	to make peace (with)
el pacificador	peacekeeper
las fuerzas de pacificación	peacekeeping force
en tiempo de paz	in peacetime
el apaciguamiento	appeasement
apaciguar	to appease
firmar un tratado	to sign a treaty
abogar por un cese de hostilidades	to call for an end to hostilities
disuadir	to deter
un arma disuasiva	deterrent weapon
el movimiento de paz	peace movement
el pacifismo	pacifism
ser pacifista	to be a pacifist
la manifestación pacifista	peace demonstration
aspirar por una solución negociada	to seek a negotiated solution
hacer una campaña antimilitarista	to carry out an anti-military campaign
el alto el fuego/el cese de hostilidades	ceasefire
'dad una oportunidad a la paz'	'give peace a chance'

WWW. www.fut.es/~msanroma/GUERRACIVIL/guerracivil.html

El medio ambiente

El ecosistema	The ecosystem
alertar a la opinión pública	to alert public opinion
el entorno natural	natural surroundings/environment
reducir los daños causados a...	to reduce the damage caused to...
la amenaza a la naturaleza	the threat to wildlife
amenazar el equilibrio ecológico	to threaten the ecological balance
la supervivencia del hombre	man's survival
la destrucción de la capa de ozono	destruction of the ozone layer
el agujero de ozono	hole in the ozone layer
el cloroflurocarbono	chlorofluorocarbon, CFC
los hidrocarburos	hydrocarbons
las lluvias ácidas	acid rain
el recalentamiento del planeta	global warming
el efecto invernadero	greenhouse effect
las radiaciones ultravioletas	ultraviolet radiation
modificar el ecosistema	to change the ecosystem
trastornar el equilibrio ecológico	to upset the ecological balance
el aumento del nivel del mar	increase in sea level
el spray	spray, aerosol
el aerosol	aerosol
la utilización pacífica de la energía nuclear	peaceful use of nuclear energy
los residuos radioactivos	radioactive waste
los efectos nocivos	harmful effects
el deterioro ambiental	environmental damage
causar daños irreversibles	to cause irreversible damage
el empeoramiento de la calidad de la vida	reduction of the quality of life
la desertización	desertification
desatender las advertencias de los científicos	to ignore the scientists' warnings
el viento y el aire no conocen fronteras	the wind and the air know no frontiers
un planeta moribundo	a dying planet
los gases contaminantes	polluting gases
la capacidad de absorción de la naturaleza	nature's ability to absorb

los contaminantes atmosféricos	atmospheric pollutants
la contaminación atmosférica transfronteriza	cross-frontier atmospheric pollution
verter al mar	to tip into the sea
el vertedero	rubbish tip
la destrucción de las selvas tropicales	destruction of the rain forests
los países subdesarrollados	under-developed countries
luchar por la supervivencia de la especie	to fight for the survival of a species
el movimiento ecologista mundial	world ecology movement
el deterioro del medio ambiente	abuse of the environment
no exportar los contaminantes a los países en vías de desarrollo	not to export pollutants to developing countries
el ICONA (Instituto para la Conservación de la Naturaleza)	Nature Conservancy Council (*in Spain*)

B **Los recursos naturales** — **Natural resources**

el ahorro de energía	energy saving
conservar la energía	to conserve energy
el consumo de energía	energy consumption
encender/apagar la calefacción	to switch the heating on/off
dejar encendidas las luces	to leave the lights on
los recursos se agotan	resources are being exhausted
toneladas de bolsas de plástico	tons of plastic bags
los envases de cartón	cardboard packaging
la pérdida de recursos valiosos	the loss of valuable resources
el despilfarro	wastefulness, squandering
despilfarrar	to squander
conservar los recursos escasos del planeta	to conserve the planet's scarce resources
el reciclaje de los desperdicios/ la basura	recycling of waste
reciclar	to recycle
los países industrializados	industrialised countries
consumir un x% de todos los recursos del mundo	to consume x% of all the world's resources
el consumo de recursos naturales	the consumption of natural resources
agotar	to exhaust
los combustibles fósiles	fossil fuels

el petróleo	crude oil
cuando el petróleo llegue a x dólares el barril	when oil reaches x dollars a barrel
los países del Cercano Oriente	Middle Eastern countries
la crisis de petróleo	the oil crisis
el uso racional de la energía disponible	the rational use of available energy
el combustible	fuel
sacar de la tierra	to take out of the ground
satisfacer nuestras necesidades	to satisfy our needs
los adelantos técnicos	technical advances
la mayor fuente de energía utilizable	the greatest source of usable energy
tomar medidas	to take measures
las reservas sin explotar	unexploited reserves
ejercer una enorme presión sobre	to exert an enormous pressure on
una política de conservación	a conservation policy
los recursos renovables	renewable resources
la energía eólica	wind energy
aprovechar la energía de las olas	to harness the energy of the waves

La contaminación | Pollution

C

I

la basura	rubbish
producir efectos tóxicos	to have toxic effects
contaminar	to pollute, contaminate
el contaminante	pollutant
contaminar	to pollute
la descontaminación	decontamination
descontaminar	to decontaminate
los residuos radioactivos	radioactive waste
la central nuclear	nuclear power-station
ser consciente de la amenaza	to be aware of the threat
el reactor nuclear	nuclear reactor
los países nuclearizados	countries with nuclear capacity
la sociedad consumista	consumerist society
envenenar	to poison
venenoso/a	poisonous
echar humo	to pour out smoke
la mancha de petróleo	oil slick

aves marinas con su plumaje empapado de petróleo	seabirds with their feathers saturated with oil
limpiar los vertidos de petróleo	to clean up oil spills

II

el nivel sonoro máximo	maximum noise level
los trastornos auditivos	hearing disorders
no debería sobrepasar los 70 decibelios	it shouldn't go above 70 decibels
el desmadre sonoro	the appalling noise level
la insonorización	soundproofing
insonorizar una casa	to soundproof a house
el aislamiento acústico/térmico	sound/heat insulation

www.mma.es
www.conama.cl/index1.asp
www.geenpeace.es
www.tierra.org
www.wwf.es

Los problemas humanos | Human problems

I

un país tercermundista	a third-world country
los países en vías de desarrollo	the developing countries
la marginación	marginalisation
estar marginado/a	to be marginalised
explotar	to exploit
sentirse explotado/a	to feel exploited
la lucha por la supervivencia cotidiana	the struggle for daily survival
empobrecerse	to become poor, impoverished
el empobrecimiento	impoverishment
la pobreza	poverty
la desnutrición	malnutrition
estar desnutrido/a	to be malnourished
la mortalidad infantil	infant mortality
la apatía	apathy
ser apático	to be apathetic
la desesperación	despair
la autosuficiencia alimenticia	self-sufficiency as regards food, ability to feed oneself
encontrarse en condiciones cada vez más precarias	to be in an ever more precarious situation
la miseria rural	rural deprivation
el hambre endémica	endemic hunger/starvation
las enfermedades relacionadas con la sequía	drought-related diseases
envejecer muy pronto	to age quickly
morir de inanición/hambre	to die of starvation

II

vivir de la tierra	to live off the land
abandonar el campo	to leave the land
desplazarse a la ciudad	to move to the city
sufrir un irreversible deterioro en su forma de ser	to suffer an irreversible decline in living conditions

ser analfabeto	to be illiterate
el analfabetismo	illiteracy
mendigar	to beg
obtener unos ingresos inferiores a la media de la renta per cápita	to receive an income below the per capita average
robar para obtener víveres	to steal in order to obtain food
cobijar	to shelter, to house
desalojar	to evict
ser carne de estadística	to be just part of the statistics, statistics fodder
vivir por debajo del umbral de pobreza	to live below the poverty line
vivir en un estado de extrema necesidad	to live in a state of dire need
vivir en un cuchitril	to live in a hovel
deber el alquiler	to owe the rent
compartir (con)	to share (with)
tener una auténtica política social hacia la pobreza	to have a real social policy towards poverty
el Estado del Bienestar	the Welfare State
las manifestaciones de la pobreza	signs of poverty
las organizaciones caritativas	charity organisations
no llegar al final del mes	not to be able to manage until the end of the month
el ínfimo nivel de la educación	the abysmal level of education
los desvalidos	the underprivileged, the helpless
los desposeídos	the deprived, the have-nots
las barriadas de chabolas	shanty town(s)
la chabola	shack, shanty
el chabolismo	the problem of the 'chabolas'
no tener recursos	to have no resources
depender de las limosnas	to depend on charity
sustentar a siete u ocho niños	to support seven or eight children
el huérfano/la huérfana	orphan
el orfelinato	orphanage
soñar con cosas grandes en la capital	to dream of great things in the capital
se acabó la esperanza	there's no more hope

Los problemas económicos — Economic problems

la deuda externa	foreign debt
el deudor	debtor
el acreedor	creditor
el préstamo	loan
reducir la deuda del tercer mundo	to reduce third-world debt
atajar el crecimiento en espiral de la deuda del tercer mundo	to stem the spiralling growth of third world debt
estar agobiado por el peso de la deuda externa	to be overwhelmed by the burden of foreign debt
el hundimiento económico	economic collapse
el crecimiento económico	economic growth
el Fondo Monetario Internacional	the International Monetary Fund
malgastar el dinero	to misspend money
establecer severos planes de ajuste económico	to implement stringent plans for economic adjustment
un plan de austeridad económica	an economic austerity plan
un programa anti-inflacionario	an anti-inflationary programme
una inflación que pasa ya del 300%	inflation already above 300%
mantener el caos a raya	to keep chaos at bay
el colapso del sistema bancario mundial	the breakdown of the world banking system
el Banco Mundial	the World Bank
las riquezas naturales	natural wealth/resources
aprovechar sus propios recursos	to benefit from one's own resources

Los problemas ecológicos — Ecological problems

la desertización de la tierra	turning of land into desert
la superpoblación	over-population
el agotamiento de la tierra	soil exhaustion
la sobreexplotación	over-exploitation
la sequía	drought
aridificarse	to become arid
la erosión	erosion
la deforestación	deforestation
la conservación de los bosques	conservation of forests
las zonas forestales	forest areas
la irrigación intensiva	intensive irrigation

A

La inmigración

Immigration

el inmigrante	immigrant
inmigrar	to immigrate
el emigrante	emigrant
emigrar	to emigrate
la población inmigrante	immigrant population
proveniente del Tercer Mundo	coming from the Third World
una situación cargada de peligros	a situation charged with danger
la mano de obra barata	cheap workforce
la segunda generación	second generation
acelerar el proceso integrador	to speed up the process of integration
una riada creciente de inmigrantes clandestinos	an increasing flow of illegal immigrants
integrarse en la sociedad	to integrate into society
el trabajador invitado	guest worker, *Gastarbeiter*
vivir fuera de su país de origen	to live outside one's country of origin
residir legalmente en...	to reside legally in...
el matrimonio mixto	mixed marriage
la solicitud de asilo	application for asylum
agravar la escasez de viviendas	to aggravate the housing shortage
la concesión de la nacionalidad	granting of nationality
tras cinco años de residencia continuada	after five years' continuous residence
el país anfitrión	host country
el permiso de trabajo	work permit
el permiso de residencia	residence permit
el derecho a la ciudadanía	right to citizenship
repatriar	to repatriate
el derecho de voto	the right to vote

B

El racismo

Racism

I

una ola de racismo	a wave of racism

la agresión	aggression
la discriminación racial	racial discrimination
discriminar	to discriminate
un acto humillante	a humiliating act
humillar	to humiliate
la represión policíaca	police repression
negar los derechos del hombre	to deny human rights
pisotear los principios morales	to trample on moral principles
el racismo encubierto	hidden racism
el odio racista	race hatred
las desigualdades raciales	racial inequalities
un ciudadano de segunda categoría	a second-class citizen
la vulneración de derechos individuales	infringement of individual rights
la xenofobia	xenophobia
la extrema derecha	the extreme right
el judío/la judía	Jew
el movimiento neonazi	neonazi movement
el sentimiento antijudío	anti-Jewish feeling
el antisemitismo	anti-Semitism
el brote de racismo	outburst of racism
el ataque de carácter racista	racist attack
el atraco	mugging, hold-up
atracar	to mug, hold up
apalear	to beat up
una campaña de terror	a campaign of terror
una ley discriminatoria	a discriminating law
estar/sentirse marginado/a	to be/feel marginalised
albergar sentimientos racistas	to harbour racist feelings
el asesinato racista	racist murder
hacer algo reprobable	to do something reprehensible
un incidente racista	a racist incident
un caso conocido de racismo	a known case of racism
las cosas han empeorado	things have got worse
corregir una situación alarmante	to rectify an alarming situation
conferir cierta respetabilidad al comportamiento racista	to confer a certain respectability on racist behaviour
representar un amplio espectro social	to represent a wide spectrum of society
una escalada de la violencia racista	an escalation of racist violence
la incapacidad de vivir juntos	inability to live together

II

la minoría étnica	ethnic minority
preservar su identidad cultural	to retain one's cultural identity
el patrimonio cultural	cultural heritage
la eliminación de todas formas de racismo	elimination of all forms of racism
ser receptivo a la diversidad cultural	to be open to cultural diversity
las ventajas de vivir en una sociedad multiracial	the benefits of living in a multiracial society

 www.arrakis.es/~jre

Las relaciones internacionales

La diplomacia	Diplomacy

A

el protocolo	protocol
la diplomacia	diplomacy
diplomático/a	diplomatic
la ONU (Organización de las Naciones Unidas)	UN (United Nations)
la Asamblea General	the General Assembly
las relaciones hispano-británicas	Anglo-Spanish relations
un acuerdo bilateral	a bilateral agreement
la política exterior	foreign policy
la inversión extranjera	foreign investment
invertir	to invest
el indicador económico	economic indicator
la internacionalización de la economía	the internationalisation of the economy
la multinacional extranjera	foreign multinational (*company*)
los intereses nacionales	national interests
la presencia extranjera	foreign presence
el Ministerio de Asuntos Exteriores	Foreign Office
el Ministerio de Defensa	Ministry of Defence
el ministro de Asuntos Exteriores	Foreign Secretary

La Unión Europea (UE)	The European Union (EU)

B

el Tratado de Roma	Treaty of Rome
solicitar la adhesión a la UE	to apply for membership of the EU
el Pacto de Adhesión	Membership Pact
el ingreso de España en la UE	the entry of Spain into the EU
las negociaciones	negotiations
negociar	to negotiate
renunciar a una parte de su soberanía	to give up a degree of sovereignty
eliminar las barreras	to break down barriers
la libertad de la circulación de mercancías (de personas, capitales)	freedom of movement of goods (people, capital)
la competencia libre	free competition

el impuesto sobre el valor añadido (IVA)	Value Added Tax (VAT)
la unión aduanera	customs union
el Parlamento Europeo	the European Parliament
el Banco Europeo de Inversiones	the European Investment Bank
el desarrollo regional	regional development
el aumento de las importaciones	increase in imports
la competencia europea	European competition
la integración en Europa	integration into Europe
la modernización de estructuras	modernisation of structures
modernizar	to modernise
la homologación de instituciones	standardisation of institutions
la subida general de precios alimenticios	general rise in food prices
una mayor renta agraria	a greater agricultural income
la flota pesquera española	the Spanish fishing fleet
el desarrollo industrial	industrial development
la libertad de movimiento	freedom of movement
la ampliación del mercado nacional	increasing the national market
el rendimiento exigido por la UE	performance required by the EU
protegerse del impacto del cambio	to protect oneself from the effects of change
los productores	producers
el monopolio	monopoly
el convenio	agreement
el Consejo de Europa	Council of Europe
el diputado europeo	member of the European Parliament
los países miembros	member countries
el funcionario	civil servant
la compañía exportadora/ importadora	export/import company
Europa occidental	western Europe
ingresar en el Mercado Común	to join the Common Market
el incremento del coste de la vida	increase in the cost of living
el pasaporte comunitario	Community passport
el consumidor español	the Spanish consumer
el período transitorio	transition period
adaptarse a la competencia comunitaria	to adapt to Community-wide competition
ampliar sus gamas de productos	to widen one's range of products

homologar los niveles de calidad	to standardise quality levels
un abaratamiento para el consumidor	a price cut for the consumer
la supresión de barreras proteccionistas	the abolition of protectionist barriers
las barreras aduaneras	customs barriers
la apertura oficial de las negociaciones	the official opening of negotiations
PIB (Producto Interior Bruto)	GNP (Gross National Product)
el movimiento de trabajadores	the movement of workers
el arancel	customs tariff
el desarme arancelario	removal of tariff barriers
firmar un acuerdo de cooperación	to sign a cooperation agreement
los efectos de la adhesión	the effects of joining (the EU)
hacer frente al desafío de la adhesión	to face up to the challenge of membership
el sistema monetario europeo (SME)	European monetary system (EMS)
una moneda común	a common currency
la unidad de cuenta europea (el ECU)	European currency unit (ECU)
el estreno del euro	the launch of the euro
la eurozona	Eurozone, Euroland
la cesta de monedas	the basket of currencies
la armonización de las políticas económicas	harmonisation of economic policies
una mayor estabilidad	a greater stability
la política agrícola común (PAC)	common agricultural policy (CAP)
la sobreexplotación de los recursos del mar	over-exploitation of the sea's resources
la conservación y la gestión de los recursos	conservation and management of resources
la estrategia energética común	common energy strategy
la igualdad de oportunidades para todos los cuidadanos europeos	equality of opportunity for all European citizens
los retos para el futuro	challenges for the future

La OTAN

NATO

la Organización del Tratado del Atlántico del Norte	North Atlantic Treaty Organisation

el secretario general	general secretary
permanecer en la Alianza Atlántica	to remain in the Atlantic Alliance
integrarse en la estructura militar de mando	to become part of the military command structure
la situación de seguridad	the security situation
los aliados	the allies
la defensa de Europa	the defence of Europe
la pérdida de la libertad de acción	loss of freedom of action
los objetivos militares	military objectives
el Pacto de Varsovia	Warsaw Pact
en la epoca de la guerra fría	at the time of the Cold War
la carrera de armamentos	arms race
los países no alineados	the non-aligned countries
el valor estratégico de España	Spain's strategic value
la importancia militar	military importance
supeditar la libertad de acción a la OTAN	to subordinate freedom of action to NATO
firmar un acuerdo mutuo de defensa	to sign a mutual defence agreement
deshacerse de las bases norteamericanas	to get rid of American bases
la presencia militar	military presence
la cumbre	summit (meeting)
el equilibrio militar	military balance
el desequilibrio	imbalance
el presupuesto defensivo	the defence budget

D

Gibraltar

Gibraltar

el Peñón	the Rock (– *Gibraltar*)
gibraltareño/a	Gibraltarian
el llanito/la llanita	Gibraltarian (*coll.*)
las autoridades	the authorities
levantar restricciones	to lift restrictions
abrir la verja	to open the frontier gate
la apertura de la verja	the opening of the frontier
la colonia británica	British colony
el contencioso de Gibraltar	the argument over Gibraltar
demostrar una capacidad de compromiso	to show a capacity for compromise
las discusiones concluyeron sin acuerdo	the discussions ended without an agreement

la soberanía del Peñón	the sovereignty of the Rock
a través de los canales diplomáticos ordinarios	through normal diplomatic channels
la devolución de Gibraltar a España	the return of Gibraltar to Spain
resolver el problema de Gibraltar	to solve the Gibraltar problem
ceder el Peñón	to give up the Rock
la importancia estratégica	strategic importance
una soberanía compartida	shared sovereignty
recuperar Gibraltar	to regain, get Gibraltar back
la frontera terrestre	the land frontier
la seguridad del Estrecho	the security of the Strait
el paraíso fiscal	tax haven
considerar los aspectos militares y estratégicos	to consider the military and strategic aspects
los aduaneros españoles están en paro técnico	the Spanish Customs are working to rule
los gibraltareños no quieren someterse a la soberanía española	the Gibraltarians don't want to submit to Spanish rule

www.un.org./spanish
www.pagina.de/deuda_externa
www.euroinfo.cce.es
www.europarl.es

La democracia

Democracy

I

elegir	to elect
el partido	party
los máximos dirigentes del partido	the top party leaders
el líder	leader
bajo el liderazgo de Felipe González	under the leadership of Felipe González
un gobierno encabezado por Aznar	a government headed by Aznar
gobernar	to govern
un gobierno de izquierdas/derechas	a left-wing/right-wing government
derechista	right-wing (*adj.*)
izquierdista	left-wing (*adj.*)
el comunismo	communism
comunista	communist
el socialismo	socialism
socialista	socialist
un gobierno laborista	a labour government
el partido centrista	centre party
el conservadurismo	conservatism
conservador	conservative
el poder político	political power
el grupo político	political group
la agrupación política	political grouping
el político	politician
la política	politics; policy
el ala (*f*) derecha del partido	the right wing of the party
la clase media alta/baja	the upper/lower middle class
con el apoyo de la clase obrera	with working-class support
apoyar	to support
el Congreso de los Diputados	the Congress of Deputies (*House of Commons*)
el Parlamento	Parliament
las Cortes	(Spanish) Parliament
la Cámara	Chamber

la Cámara de los Comunes	House of Commons
la Cámara de los Lores	House of Lords
el debate	debate
el discurso	speech
la réplica	reply
la oposición	the opposition
la polémica	discussion, argument, polemic
el presidente del gobierno	president, prime minister
el primer ministro/la primera ministra	prime minister
por motivos políticos	for political motives/reasons

II

la campaña electoral	election campaign
las elecciones generales	general election
ganar 100 escaños	to win 100 (*parliamentary*) seats
el voto	vote
votar (por los socialistas)	to vote (for the socialists)
las urnas	ballot boxes
ir a las urnas	to go to the polls
el referéndum	referendum
el portavoz	spokesperson
lograr el objetivo de sacar a España adelante	to achieve the objective of moving Spain forward
las fuerzas de orden público	the forces of public order
los derechos humanos	human rights
salvaguardar las libertades y los derechos del pueblo	to safeguard the freedoms and rights of the people
la actitud política	political attitude
el boicot	boycott
boicotear	to boycott

La dictadura

Dictatorship

el régimen	regime
el franquismo	Francoism, politics of the Franco regime
en la época franquista	in Franco's time
el dictador	dictator
la dictadura	dictatorship

B

81

el Caudillo	fascist leader (*esp. with reference to Franco*)
el fascismo	fascism
fascista	fascist
el facha	derogatory slang term for fascist
ultraderechista	extreme right-wing
el golpe de estado	*coup d'état*
el golpismo	coup mentality
el golpista	one who takes part in a coup
el gobierno títere	puppet government

C La violencia política   Political violence

I

derrocar el gobierno	to bring down the government
el cuartelazo	military uprising, army coup
el golpe militar	military coup
las operaciones guerrilleras	guerrilla operations
la violencia terrorista	terrorist violence
las organizaciones internacionales de derechos humanos	international human rights organisations
los desaparecidos violentamente	those who have disappeared by force
la desaparición de una persona	a person's disappearance
mantener vivo el sistema democrático	to keep the democratic system alive
la corrupción de los políticos	political corruption
corromper	to corrupt
corrompido/a	corrupt
hundirse en la guerra civil	to plunge into civil war
evitar una guerra civil	to avoid a civil war
las matanzas colectivas	mass killings
la masacre sangrienta	bloody massacre
el atentado	outrage; attempt on someone's life
el asesinato político	political assassination/murder
ahogarse en sangre	to drown in blood
matar por matar	to kill for the sake of killing
secuestrar	to kidnap
firmar una tregua	to sign a truce
romper una tregua	to break a truce
la ruptura de una tregua	the breaking of a truce

atreverse a protestar	to dare to protest
la ley del patrón	the law of the rich owner/boss
estar sobrecogido/a por el terror	to be cowed by terror
crear continuos conflictos	to create continual conflicts
la canción de protesta	protest song
'el pueblo unido jamás será vencido'	'the people united will never be defeated'

II

el terrorismo	terrorism
el/la terrorista	terrorist
la organización terrorista	terrorist organisation
el grupo terrorista	terrorist group
el simpatizante	sympathiser
el grupo separatista	separatist group
ETA (Euskadi Ta Askatasuna)	ETA (Basque separatist group)
etarra	member of, or to do with, ETA
el atentado con bomba	bomb outrage
el coche bomba	car bomb
la bomba de relojería	booby-trap bomb
el atentado terrorista	terrorist outrage
asesinar	to murder
el asesinato	murder
quitarle la vida a alguien	to take someone's life
mutilar	to maim
lesionar	to injure
herir	to wound
una célula del IRA	an IRA cell
el/la victima	victim
el explosivo Semtex	Semtex explosive
volar una fábrica	to blow up a factory
desactivar una bomba	to defuse a bomb
el artificiero/experto en desactivar explosivos	bomb disposal expert
tomar a una persona como rehén	to take someone hostage
los rehenes detenidos en Chechniá	the hostages held in Chechnya
la guerra de guerrillas	guerrilla warfare
los rebeldes	the rebels
la sublevación	uprising
la revolución	revolution
revolucionario	revolutionary

los disturbios callejeros	street riots
tener el apoyo del gobierno	to have the support of the government
luchar por la independencia	to struggle/fight for independence
entregar su vida por	to give up one's life for

D La monarquía

Monarchy

I

ser monárquico	to be a monarchist
el/la monarca	monarch
el/la soberano/a	sovereign
los Reyes de España	King and Queen of Spain
el Príncipe de Asturias	Prince of Asturias
la Infanta Elena	Princess Elena
la corona española	the Spanish crown
la Familia Real	Royal Family
la Zarzuela	*home of Spanish royal family*
el presupuesto anual	annual budget
el Jefe del Estado	Head of State
la coronación	coronation
las obligaciones oficiales	official duties
desde un punto de vista (anti-) monárquico...	from (an anti-monarchist) point of view...
durante el reinado de Alfonso XIII	during the reign of Alfonso XIII
el Reino Unido	United Kingdom
reinar	to reign
goza de un prestigio sin parangón	he enjoys unequalled prestige
la Constitución de 1978	the 1978 Constitution
el sistema constitucional	constitutional system
mantenerse por encima de la política cotidiana	to remain above everyday politics
cumplir con su deber	to fulfil one's duty
romper el protocolo	to break protocol
hacerse querer por todos	to be loved by all
el protagonista de la transición democrática	the leader of the transition to democracy
jugar un papel primordial en el cambio hacia la democracia	to play a fundamental role in the change to democracy
las cuestiones protocolarias	matters of protocol
tener sangre real	to have royal blood

ofrecer estabilidad	to offer stability
el jefe de las Fuerzas Armadas	chief of the armed forces

II

estar en contra de la monarquía	to be against the monarchy
gozar del privilegio	to enjoy privilege
privilegiado/a	privileged
gozar del poder hereditario	to enjoy hereditary power
disfrutar de la riqueza heredada	to enjoy inherited (unearned) wealth
debería trabajar como cualquier hijo/a de vecino	he/she should have to work like any other citizen
pagar los impuestos	to pay taxes

Las autonomías / The self-governing regions

E

el gobierno regional	regional government
el deseo autonómico	desire for regional government
el autogobierno	self-government
la Comunidad Autónoma	self-governing region (*of Spain*)
reconocer el derecho a la autonomía	to recognise the right to self-government
tener una lengua propia	to have one's own language
suscitar expectativas	to awaken expectations
esto no supone una panacea para...	this does not imply a panacea for...
crear conflictos sociales	to create social conflict
crear más burocracia	to create more bureaucracy
se tiende a una Europa sin fronteras	there is a tendency to a Europe without frontiers
la lengua catalana	the Catalan language
la Generalitat	Catalan Parliament
los vascos	the Basques
el País Vasco ⎫ Euskadi ⎭	the Basque Country
el euskera	Basque (*language*)

www. www.casareal.es/casareal/home.html

La economía y los negocios

A

La economía	The economy
la economía dirigida	planned economy
la economía del mercado	market economy
el centro bancario y financiero mundial	world banking and financial centre
el sector público	public sector
el sector privado	private sector
privatizar	to privatise
la privatización	privatisation
fomentar el capital privado	to encourage private capital
nacionalizar	to nationalise
la nacionalización	nationalisation
subvencionar	to subsidise
la subvención	subsidy
el mercado de cambio de monedas	foreign exchange market
tras años de estancamiento	after years of stagnation
el despegue de le economía española	the lift-off of the Spanish economy
las actividades económicas	economic activities
el presupuesto	budget
el consumidor	consumer
el consumismo	consumerism
la sociedad consumista	the consumer society
los bienes de consumo	consumer goods
el poder adquisitivo	purchasing power
la cesta de la compra	shopping basket
Hacienda	Treasury, Exchequer
el Ministro de Hacienda	Chancellor of the Exchequer
la Bolsa	Stock Exchange
el agene de Bolsa	stockbroker
las acciones	shares
el/la accionista	shareholder
la deuda nacional	the national debt
el ahorro	savings
la Caja de Ahorros	savings bank
ahorrar	to save
la balanza de pagos	balance of payments

la banca	the banks (*collectively*)
el banco	bank (*building*)
el cambio	exchange
la devaluación	devaluation
devaluar/revaluar la peseta	to devalue/revalue the peseta
las divisas extranjeras	foreign exchange, currency
la estadística	statistic(s)
la hipoteca	mortgage
hipotecar	to mortgage
el impuesto sobre la renta	income tax
el impuesto sobre el valor añadido (IVA)	value added tax (VAT)
bruto	gross
neto	net
combatir la inflación	to combat inflation
la tasa de la inflación	inflation rate
la espiral inflacionista	the spiral of inflation
invertir capital en España	to invest capital in Spain
la inversión	investment
la libre competencia	free competition
el mercado libre	free market
estar sujeto a las fuerzas del mercado	to be subject to market forces
la plusvalía	appreciation, capital gains
el préstamo	loan
prestar	to lend
los movimientos bancarios	bank movements
la fluctuación de los tipos de interés	interest rate fluctuation
un alza (f) en los tipos de interés	a rise in interest rates
simplificar los trámites aduaneros	to simplify customs formalities
la tarjeta de crédito	credit card
el cajero automático	automatic cash dispenser
pedir el saldo	to ask for a balance statement

Los negocios

Business

la empresa	firm, company
la (empresa) subsidiaria	subsidiary, branch
los recursos	resources
las posibilidades de desarrollo	development possibilities

B

el acreedor	creditor
el beneficio	profit
la contabilidad	accounting
el/la contable	accountant
la cooperativa	cooperative
el convenio	agreement, accord
la venta al detalle/al por menor	retail sale
la venta al por mayor	wholesale
la entidad	company, organisation
el contrato multimillonario	multimillion contract
las cifras de exportación	export figures
la importación	import
financiar un proyecto	to finance a project
la fusión de dos empresas	merger of two companies
mantener la liquidez	to maintain liquidity, solvency
el margen de beneficio	profit margin
la mercancía	goods, merchandise
un negocio rentable	a profitable business
la rentabilidad	profitability
el pago	payment
las pérdidas	losses
la planificación	planning
planificar	to plan
incrementar la productividad	to increase productivity
la renta	income, revenue
el riesgo	risk
arriesgar	to risk
la venta a plazos	sale by instalments

www.worldbank.org/html/extdr/espanol
www.bolsa-actual.com

La religión

20

I

abrazar el cristianismo	to embrace Christianity
ser cristiano/a	to be a Christian
Jesús/Jesucristo	Jesus/Jesus Christ
el Padre, el Hijo y el Espíritu Santo	Father, Son and Holy Ghost
la Virgen María	the Virgin Mary
según la (Santa) Biblia	according to the (Holy) Bible
predicar el Evangelio	to preach the Gospel
el Catolicismo	Catholicism
la Iglesia Católica	the Catholic Church
el Papa	Pope
el Protestantismo	Protestantism
ser protestante	to be a protestant
crucificar	to crucify
la crucifixión	crucifixion
la ortodoxia religiosa	religious orthodoxy
el obispo de Sevilla	the Bishop of Seville
el arzobispo de Toledo	the Archbishop of Toledo
el cura	priest
el sacerdote	priest
el párroco	parish priest
la parroquia	parish, parish church
el santo/la santa	saint
rezar	to pray
las oraciones	prayers
bautizar a un niño	to christen, baptise a child
casarse por la iglesia	to get married in church
ir a misa	to go to mass
el oficio	service
el culto	worship
la Primera Comunión	First Communion
la Confirmación	Confirmation
la virginidad	virginity
el nacimiento sin mancha	virgin birth
la resurrección	resurrection
el fanatismo religioso	religious fanaticism, bigotry
las matanzas sectarias	sectarian killings
el infierno	hell
el culto del diablo	devil worship

Satanás   Satan
practicar el satanismo   to practise satanism

II

el Islam   Islam
musulmán   Muslim
Alá   Allah
el profeta Mahoma   the prophet Mohammed
la mezquita   mosque
el Corán   Koran
el fundamentalismo islámico   Islamic fundamentalism
el Judaísmo   Judaism
judío   Jew, Jewish
sionista   Zionist
el Hinduismo   Hinduism
el Budismo   Buddhism

III

practicar una religión   to practise a religion
dar sentido a la vida   to give meaning to life
creer en Dios   to believe in God
ser creyente   to be a believer
ser católico/a practicante   to be a practising Catholic
profesar una fe   to profess a faith
ser ateo/a   to be an atheist
el ateísmo   atheism
ser agnóstico/a   to be an agnostic
la (in)tolerancia religiosa   religious (in)tolerance
rechazar   to reject
ser escéptico/a   to be sceptical
no me hace nada la religión   religion does nothing for me
manifestarse de acuerdo con el Papa   to come out in favour of the Pope
sentir un vacío   to feel a gap/an emptiness
el milagro   miracle
tener/sentir una vocación religiosa   to have/feel a religious vocation
la deidad   deity
la diosa   goddess
fallecer   to die, pass away
después de morir   after death
la muerte   death
irse al otro barrio   to 'snuff it' (coll.)
el otro mundo   the other world, next world

La informática

I

la revolución informática	information technology revolution
el ordenador	computer
el ordenador portátil	laptop computer
informatizar	to computerise
el chip	chip
la pantalla	screen, VDU
el monitor	monitor
el disco duro	hard disk
el disquete	floppy disk
el disco compacto	compact disc
la unidad de disco	disk drive
la potencia	power
el software	software
el teclado	keyboard
la tecla	key (of keyboard)
teclear	to type
la barra espaciadora	space bar
el tabulador	tabulator
el joystick	joystick
el ratón	mouse
pulsar	to press (key), click (mouse)
pulsar dos veces	to double click
el cursor	cursor
mover el cursor	to move the cursor
hacer aparecer el menú	to call up the menu
procesar	to process
el procesador de textos	word processor
programar	to program
el programador/la programadora	programmer
el archivo	file
archivar	to save
editar	to edit
arrastrar	to drag
pegar	to paste
suprimir/eliminar/borrar	to delete

acceder al sistema	to log on
la clave de acceso	password
el acceso a la información	access to information
la conexión de redes	networking
el pirata informático	hacker
salir del sistema	to log off
abrir/cerrar una ventana	to open/close a window
la imagen (pl imágenes)	picture
almacenar	to store
el almacenamiento de datos	data storage
la base/el banco de datos	database/bank
la ley de protección de datos	data protection law
comprobar la ortografía	to spellcheck
la copia de seguridad	back-up copy
el disquete de reserva	back-up disk
bloquearse	to crash
al pulsar un botón	at the push of a button
la impresora	printer
encender la impresora	to switch the printer on
imprimir	to print, print out
el listado	printout
la impresora de inyección de tinta a color	ink jet colour printer
el sistema de impresión inyección de burbujas	bubble jet printing system
la impresora láser	laser printer
la fuente	font
el escáner	scanner
de alto rendimiento	(of) high performance
apagar	to switch off

II

Internet	the Internet
la red	the Web
la web	the Web; also: Website
la superautopista	superhighway
la página web	Web page
conectarse con	to connect/link up with
accederse a la red	to access the web
el costo de la conexión a Internet	the cost of Internet connection
el módem	modem

navegar	to surf (*i.e. the web*)
el/la navegante *or* el/la internauta	(web) surfer
buscar	to search
el buscador	search (*i.e. the equipment*)
la búsqueda	search (*i.e. the action*)
el correo electrónico	e-mail (*i.e. the system*)
mandar por correo electrónico	to send by e-mail, to e-mail
el e-mail	e-mail (*i.e. the document sent or received*)
la dirección	address
descargar	to download
eliminar un virus	to get rid of a virus

III

transformar la cultura humana	to transform/change human culture
el desarrollo científico	scientific development
desarrollar	to develop
los adelantos tecnológicos	technological advances
una sociedad evolucionada	a developed society
la innovación técnica	technical innovation
aprovechar los adelantos científicos	to benefit from scientific advances
asimilar las nuevas tecnologías	to assimilate the new technologies
transmitir e intercambiar información	to transmit and exchange information
ahorrar tiempo y dinero	to save time and money
nuevos recursos para los directivos	new resources for management
trabajar con más eficacia	to work more effectively
contribuir a las estadísticas del paro	to contribute to the unemployment statistics

Para nuestra comodidad	**For our convenience**
el aparato	apparatus, machine, gadget
el equipo	equipment
los electrodomésticos	electrical appliances for the home
el equipo de hi-fi	hi-fi equipment
el sintonizador digital	digital tuner
sintonizar	to tune (in)
el disco compacto, CD	compact disc, CD (*disc or player*)

B

el lector de CD	CD player
la fotocopiadora	photocopier
fotocopiar	to photocopy
la fotocopia	photocopy
el teléfono inalámbrico	cordless phone
el teléfono portátil	mobile phone
el facsímile/fax	facsimile/fax
mandar por fax	to fax
¿puede faxeármelo?	can you fax it to me?
el magnetofón	tape recorder
el vídeo	video, video recorder
el videograbadora	video recorder
grabar	to record
el horno microondas	microwave oven
el televisor	television set
el mando a distancia	remote control, zapper
la televisión por satélite/cable	satellite/cable television
la antena parabólica	satellite dish
la calculadora	calculator
el sistema de seguridad	security system
la cerradura electrónica	electronic locking
la alarma antirrobo	anti-theft alarm
la alarma antiincendios	fire alarm
activar el detector de humo	to set off the smoke detector
la caja de control	control box
el cajero automático	automatic cash dispenser
el lavaplatos	dishwasher
la lavadora	washing machine
la secadora	tumble-drier
el secador de pelo	hairdrier
la batidora	food mixer
el robot de cocina	food processor
enchufar	to plug in
desenchufar	to unplug
el enchufe	power point

C El personal, los procesos y las sustancias

People, processes and substances

I

el científico/la científica	scientist

el tecnólogo/la tecnóloga	technologist
la química	chemistry
el químico/la química	chemist
la física	physics
el físico/la física	physicist
la zoología	zoology
el zoólogo/la zoóloga	zoologist
investigar	to research
el investigador/la investigadora	researcher
promover las investigaciones científicas	to promote scientific research
seguir una línea de investigación	to follow a line of investigation
la sustancia	substance
el elemento	element
el compuesto	compound
el proceso	process
el laboratorio	laboratory
pasar por un circuito	to pass through a circuit
el oxígeno	oxygen
el hidrógeno	hydrogen
el nitrógeno	nitrogen
el monóxido/dióxido de carbono	carbon monoxide/dioxide
el mercurio	mercury
el plomo	lead
el complejo petroquímico	petrochemical complex

II

la energía nuclear	nuclear energy
radioactivo	radioactive
la central nuclear	nuclear power station
montar una campaña antinuclear	to mount an anti-nuclear campaign
una fuga de radioactividad	a radioactive leak
el siniestro nuclear	nuclear disaster
el reactor	reactor
la explosión	explosion
explotar	to explode
el contador Geiger registra...	the Geiger counter registers...
alcanzar la fusión	to reach meltdown
como consecuencia de Chernóbil	in the aftermath of Chernobyl

D

La exploración del espacio	Space exploration
La exploración del espacio	**Space exploration**
el satélite meteorológico	meteorological satellite
la longitud de onda	wavelength
poner en órbita	to put into orbit
el transbordador espacial	space shuttle
la lanzadera espacial	space launch pad
lanzar	to launch
la nave (espacial)	(space) ship
la cápsula	capsule
el satélite de comunicaciones	communications satellite
el radar	radar
el sonar	sonar

 http://btr0xw.rz.uni-bayreuth.de/solar/span/history.htm

Las artes visuales

Visual arts

A

el dibujo	drawing
dibujar	to draw
el diseño	design
diseñar	to design
la escultura	sculpture
esculpir	to sculpt
el escultor/la escultura	sculptor
la exposición	exhibition
la colección	collection
el arte abstracto	abstract art
el símbolo	symbol
simbolizar	to symbolise
representar	to represent
pintar	to paint
la pintura	painting
el pintor/la pintora	painter
pintoresco	picturesque
el cuadro	picture
el lienzo	canvas
el retrato	portrait
retratar	to portray, paint a portrait of
la acuarela	watercolour
la pintura al óleo	oil painting
pintar al óleo	to paint in oils
el bodegón	still life
representar	to depict
el pincel	paintbrush
la pincelada	brush stroke
el contraste de la luz y sombra	contrast of light and shadow
especializarse en la representación de la forma humana	to specialise in the depiction of the human form
no pertenece a ninguna escuela reconocida	he/she doesn't belong to any recognised school
tiene su estilo individual	he/she has his/her own individual style
el museo de bellas artes	fine arts museum

la galería	gallery
de la escuela impresionista	of the impressionist school
la venta	sale
vender por una cifra elevada	to sell for a high price
el lote	lot
la subasta	auction
la puja	bid
pujar	to bid
la obra maestra	masterwork, masterpiece
el aficionado	fan, enthusiast

B

El cine y el teatro	**Cinema and theatre**

I

la localidad	seat
la taquilla	box office
el actor/la actriz	actor/actress
la estrella de cine	film star
el film(e) (*pl* films or filmes)	film
la película	film
rodar una película	to shoot a film
el largometraje	full-length film , feature film
el cortometraje	'short' (film)
la pantalla	screen
el rol/el papel	role
desempeñar un papel	to play a part/role
el/la protagonista	main role, protagonist
protagonizar	to play the main part, protagonist in
una película protagonizada por X·	a film with X in the leading role
el guión	script
el guionista	scriptwriter
el director/la directora	director
el/la cineasta	film maker
doblar en castellano	to dub into Spanish
la banda sonora	sound track
los subtítulos	subtitles
la película está subtitulada en catalán	the film is subtitled in Catalan
para todos los públicos	suitable for all ages
no recomendada a menores de trece años	not suitable for under-13s
la sesión continua	continuous performance
la película en conjunto	the film as a whole
estrenar una película/una obra	to put on a film/play for the first time

el estreno	first showing/performance
la movida madrileña	the Madrid 'scene'
despertó mucho interés con su primera película	he aroused a great deal of interest with his first film
a lo largo de su carrera	throughout his/her career
explorar nuevos horizontes	to explore new horizons
gozar del cine/del teatro	to enjoy the cinema/theatre

II

la obra (de teatro)	play
poner una obra en escena	to produce a play
la puesta en escena	production
interpretar una obra	to perform/interpret a play
la interpretación	performance, interpretation
actuar	to act
la actuación	the acting
la comedia	comedy
la tragedia	tragedy
el espectáculo teatral	(theatre) show
la escena/el escenario	stage
el montaje	design, décor
la obra está ambientada en Roma	the play is set in Rome
las butacas	stalls
la trama es muy enrevesada	the plot is very involved
el desenlace	outcome, dénouement
al caer el telón	when the curtain fell
aplaudir	to applaud
los aplausos	applause
silbar	to hiss, boo
ante el público	in front of the audience
el miedo al público	stage fright
el maquillaje	make-up
maquillarse	to put one's make-up on
la temporada	season (*theatre etc*)
el teatro callejero	street theatre
los títeres	puppets
subvencionar el teatro	to subsidise the theatre
la subvención gubernamental	government subsidy
patrocinar las bellas artes	to sponsor the fine arts
bajo el patrocinio de	under the sponsorship of
contar con el apoyo del Ministerio de Cultura	to rely on the support of the Ministry of Culture

La literatura	Literature
la lectura	reading
el lector/la lectora	reader
el estilo	style
el editor	editor
el escritor/la escritora	writer
el autor/la autora	author
la biblioteca	library
el bibliotecario/la bibliotecaria	librarian
la librería	bookshop
el librero/la librera	bookseller
la tirada	edition, print run
la reproducción ilegal	illegal copying
el premio Nobel por la literatura	the Nobel Prize for literature
el libro de bolsillo	paperback
la novela	novel
el cuento	short story, tale
el/la cuentista	short story writer
la (auto)biografía	(auto)biography
(auto)biográfico/a	(auto)biographical
la novela policíaca	detective novel
es un/a apasionado/a de la ciencia-ficción	he/she is a science fiction addict
la narración	narrative
la historia se localiza en Madrid	the story is set in Madrid
el desenlace es una verdadera sorpresa	the outcome is a real surprise
saber contar una historia	to know how to tell a story, be a good storyteller
el cuento alcanza su desenlace	the story unfolds
el/la escritor/a de vanguardia	avant-garde writer
la casa editorial	publishing firm
el género	genre
los derechos de autor	royalties
ser ratón de biblioteca	to be a bookworm
disfrutar de una buena lectura	to enjoy a good read
en toda su obra	in the whole of his/her work
la poesía	poetry; poem
la obra poética	poetic work

D

La música

Music

la sala de conciertos	concert hall
el auditorio	concert hall, auditorium
la orquesta de cámara	chamber orchestra
la orquesta filarmónica	philharmonic orchestra
el coro	choir
el compositor/la compositora	composer
componer	to compose
la partitura	score (*musical*)
la quinta sinfonía de Beethoven	Beethoven's fifth symphony
una gran obra sinfónica	a great symphonic work
el concierto en si bemol menor de Chaikovski	Tchaikovsky's B flat minor concerto
la ópera	opera
el aria (f) operática	operatic aria
el/la cantante	singer
el cantaor/la cantaora	flamenco singer (*only*)
el cantautor/la cantautora	singer-songwriter
cantar	to sing
el músico/la música	musician, player
el/la instrumentalista	instrumentalist
el/la solista	soloist
ser clarinetista	to be a clarinettist
tocar la flauta	to play the flute
el director/la directora	conductor
la orquesta fue dirigida por...	the orchestra was conducted by...
bajo la batuta de...	under the baton of...
el primer violín	leader, first violin
ser muy aficionado a Mozart	to be very fond of Mozart
tocar la música en la calle	to busk
el músico ambulante	busker
la música pop	pop music
el conjunto de pop	pop group
el rockero/la rockera	rock singer, rock fan
el sencillo	single (disc)
el elepé	LP (long-play record)
el CD, disco compacto	CD, compact disc

La crítica

Criticism

el crítico de teatro/cine/música	theatre/film/music critic
se criticó de lento y pesado	it was criticised as slow and tedious

E

¡dos horas de carcajadas!	two hours of laughter!
logra que el público ría de principio al fin	s/he manages to get the audience laughing from beginning to end
mantener la tensión a lo largo de toda la representación	to keep up the tension throughout the performance
es todo un espectáculo	it's quite a show
la brillante interpretación de los actores	the brilliant performance by the actors
demuestra su calidad de primer/a actor/actriz	he/she demonstrates his/her skill as a first-rate actor/actress
el secreto del gran actor	the secret of the great actor
fue un fracaso total	it was an utter flop
fracasar	to fail, flop
es una película...	it is a ...... film
sobresaliente	outstanding
exigente	demanding
esotérica	esoteric/highbrow
enrevesada	involved
pesada	tedious
ligera	light
salada	witty
humorística	humorous, funny
deprimente	depressing
amena	pleasant
chocarrera	scurrilous
satírica	satirical
se publicó en	it was published in
se estrenó en	it was first shown/performed in
analizar	to analyse
citar	to quote
la citación	quotation
al leer/ver esta escena	when I read/saw this scene
mi primera reacción fue (+ *noun* or *inf*)	my first reaction was (+ *noun* or *to*...)
me encantó la yuxtaposición de... y...	I loved the juxtaposition of... and...
el uso de la poesía/del baile	the use of poetry/dance
de esto se puede inferir que...	from this we can infer that...
está escrito en prosa	it is written in prose
tiene un estilo muy lírico	s/he has a very lyrical style

www.softguides.com/index_madrid.html
www.uchile.cl/actividades_culturales
www.sinadic.gov.ve
www.portal.arts.ve

The following is a selection of – mainly abstract – verbs which cannot be listed under particular topic headings but are very useful in written and spoken argument.

abolish	eliminar, suprimir
accuse	acusar
get accustomed to	acostumbrarse a
achieve	conseguir
acknowledge (*recognise*)	reconocer
act (*other than in theatre*)	actuar, obrar
add	añadir
admit	{ admitir (*all senses*) { confesar (*confess*)
advise	aconsejar
afford	costear
agree to	consentir en, quedar en
agree with	ponerse/estar de acuerdo con
allow	permitir
alter /change	cambiar
annoy	fastidiar, enojar
apologise	disculparse
appear (*seem*)	parecer
(*come into sight*)	aparecer
appreciate	apreciar (*most senses*)
	valorar (*value*)
approve	aprobar
argue (*quarrel*)	discutir, reñir
argue (*reason*)	argumentar, razonar
assist /help	ayudar
assume	asumir
assure	asegurar
attempt	intentar, probar
attract	atraer
avenge (oneself)	vengar(se)
avoid	evitar
balance	equilibrar
bear, endure	aguantar

A

B

become	hacerse (+ *noun*) llegar a ser (+ *noun*) ponerse (+ *adj*)
or convert adjective to verb	e.g. gordo → engordar
behave	comportarse
betray	traicionar
blame	culpar
boast	jactarse
borrow	pedir prestado
burn (*consume or damage by fire*)	quemar
(*be on fire*)	arder
cancel	anular
cheat (*deceive*)	burlar
check	comprobar
choose	escoger, elegir
command	mandar, ordenar
compel	obligar
complain	quejarse, lamentarse
compose	componer
conclude	concluir
confess	confesar
confuse	confundir
congratulate (on)	felicitar (por)
dare (to)	atreverse a, osar
deal (*with something*)	tratar de
decrease, diminish	disminuir
demand	exigir, reivindicar
deny	negar
depend (on)	depender (de)
deserve	merecer
despise	despreciar
develop	desarrollar
disagree (*object*)	no estar de acuerdo, oponerse
disagree (*quarrel*)	reñir, discutir
disappoint	decepcionar
disgust	dar asco
distrust	**desconfiar de, recelar**
emphasise	subrayar
endure	aguantar
enjoy	disfrutar de

envy	**envidiar**
excuse	**perdonar**
fail	**fracasar**
favour	**favorecer**
fear	**temer**
fight (for)	**luchar (por)**
forbid	**prohibir**
foresee	**prever**
forget	**olvidar**
forgive	**perdonar**
frighten	**asustar, dar susto a**
fulfil	**cumplir**
govern	**gobernar**
grumble (*about*)	**protestar (de)**
hasten	**apresurarse**
hate	**odiar, aborrecer**
hesitate	**dudar, vacilar**
hinder	**impedir, estorbar**
imagine	**imaginarse, figurarse**
improve	**mejorar**
increase	**aumentar**
influence	**influir en**
intend to	**pensar**
interrupt	**interrumpir**
judge	**juzgar**
loathe	**aborrecer**
maintain	**mantener**
manage to	**conseguir, lograr**
measure	**medir**
make a mistake (*be wrong*)	**equivocarse**
mistrust	**desconfiar de**
mix	**mezclar**
neglect	**descuidar, desatender**
notice	**observar, notar**
obey	**obedecer**
object to	**oponerse a**
offend	**ofender**
offer	**ofrecer**
omit	**omitir**
owe	**deber**
own	**poseer, ser dueño de**

F

G

H

I

J

L

M

N

O

P

permit	permitir
persuade to	persuadir a
possess	poseer
postpone	aplazar
prejudice	perjudicar
pretend (*make believe*)	fingir
prevent	impedir
profit from	aprovechar de
promise	prometer
propose	proponer
protect	proteger
prove	comprobar
provide	proveer, suministrar

Q

quarrel	reñir

R

recognise	reconocer
reflect, think	reflexionar
refuse (to)	negarse (a), rehusar
regret (*be sorry for*)	sentir, lamentar
reject	rechazar
rely on	contar con, fiarse de
require	exigir
resemble	parecerse a

S

satisfy	satisfacer
scorn	desdeñar, despreciar
succeed, be successful	tener éxito
succeed in	conseguir, lograr
suit	convenir a
supply /provide	suministrar
support	apoyar
suppose	suponer
suspect (of)	sospechar (de)

T

thank	agradecer
threaten (to/with)	amenazar (+ *infin or noun*)
trust	fiarse de

W

waste (*money/resources*)	malgastar, despilfarrar
worry	inquietarse, preocuparse

Vanguardista = revolutionary

logró = alcanzó =